DEATH ON A DISTANT FRONTIER

By the same author:

Bloody Aachen

Massacre at Malmédy

Hitler's Werewolves

The End of the War

Hunters from the Sky

A Bridge at Arnhem

Decision at St Vith

The Battle for Twelveland

Operation Africa

The Three-Star Blitz

Forty-Eight Hours to Hammelburg

The Battle of the Ruhr Pocket

The Hunt for Martin Bormann

The War in the Shadows

Operation Stalag

The Battle of Hurtgen Forest

The March on London

Operation Northwind

Bounce the Rhine

Siegfried: The Nazi's Last Stand

The Last Assault

DEATH ON A DISTANT FRONTIER

A Lost Victory, 1944
by
Charles Whiting

SOLDIERS OF THE WEST FRONT! I expect
you to defend the sacred soil of
Germany . . . to the very last! Heil Hitler.
Field Marshal von Rundstedt, 1944

'The whole art of war consists of
guessing what is on the other
side of the hill'.
The Duke of Wellington

LEO COOPER
LONDON

First published in Great Britain in 1996 by
Leo Cooper
190 Shaftesbury Avenue, London WC2H 8JL
an imprint of
Pen & Sword Books
47 Church Street, Barnsley, South Yorkshire, S70 2AS

ISBN 0 85052 517 9

A CIP record for this book is
available from the British Library

Typeset by Phoenix Typesetting,
Ilkley, West Yorkshire

Printed in England by
Redwood Books.

FOR JO

CONTENTS

ACKNOWLEDGEMENTS

I would like to express my thanks for assistance with this book to Mr R. Barrett, Mr H. Fielding, Mrs Barbara Bramall, Mr M. Tolhurst, Mr Hy Schorr, Professor Hobie Morris, Mr C. Boykin, Mr E. Taylor and M Erich Marcks. Above all I would like to thank my friend and fellow veteran, Tom Dickinson and the New York Public Library without whom this book would not have been possible.

C.W.

AUTHOR'S NOTE

Far away to the north, where Patton had just broken through and was driving hell-for-leather for the Rhine, the night sky flickered red at regular intervals. Over the waiting American line an occasional flare sailed into the air, bathing all below in its sickly light.

'The night of 19 March was quiet and peaceful,' Colonel Wallace Cheves, whose battalion of the US 70th Infantry Division would soon go into action, recalled after the war. 'The warming winds swept in from the south and sent patterns of ripples twinkling on the river.' In foxholes along the shore the men looked up at the sky and waited.

It was nearly dawn on this Tuesday, 20 March, 1945. Cheves's 'Trailblazers', as the men of the 70th were nicknamed, were about to attack the Siegfried Line on the other side of the River Saar – the 'Great Wall of Germany' which Hitler had had built nearly a decade earlier. Back in 1944 when American troops had first penetrated the Siegfried Line on the afternoon of Tuesday, 11 September, the Trailblazers had still been training some five thousand miles away from this distant frontier. Indeed some of the men now waiting tensely in their foxholes had not even been in the Army then. Those first invaders had found the Line long abandoned. The guns had vanished, dust was thick on the floors of the concrete bunkers, the barbed wire entanglements were rusty and covered with weeds and the minefields had been cleared. A local farmer had built a chicken coop outside one of the pillboxes. That afternoon it had seemed to those first invaders that the attack on the *Westwall*, as the Germans called it, would be a walkover.

That autumn victory had been in the air. The German Army in France had been shattered and the survivors were in full flight back to the Reich, a ragged, dispirited rabble. Hitler's Empire was visibly collapsing.

British troopers of the Special Air Service, who had been dropped the previous June to rally the *Maquis*, were ranging far and wide, ahead of the advancing Americans, spearheading the route and smoothing the path for the advancing armies of US Generals Hodges, Patton and Patch. Once those armies were through the abandoned Siegfried Line, there remained only one great natural barrier ahead of the Allies – the River Rhine. It seemed quite likely, as the papers back home were joyfully proclaiming, that the war would be over by Christmas! So why was it that, now, six months later, the Trailblazers and other divisions of the US Seventh Army were still attacking that Great Wall of Germany?

★   ★   ★

It is now almost thirty years since I wrote the first of a loose series of books about the fighting which I privately call 'the frontier battles'. This was *Decision at St Vith**. Since then I have attempted to cover every aspect of that six-month battle for Germany's frontier and in those three decades I must have walked along all the 350 miles of the border which divides Germany from Holland and France. On those journeys, while I've tramped the fields and forests still littered with the rusting debris of battle, I have often asked myself why it had taken the Allies so long to smash through the Siegfried Line. How had it come about that, after that terrible débâcle of September, 1944, the Germans had survived to launch the bold counter-attack of December of that year? That counter-attack, the Battle of the Bulge as it came to be known, had cost the Allies 80,000 casualties and had prolonged the fighting on that distant frontier right into March,1945. Where had the Allies' strategy failed them?

It is my opinion that the turning point in Germany's favour came during the eleven-week period between the second week of September, when that little band of Americans from the US 5th Armored Division first penetrated the Siegfried Line and 23 November when General Leclerc's 2nd Armored Division of Patch's Seventh Army captured Strasbourg and reached the Rhine.

In that second week of September, General Hodges' First Army was already penetrating the twenty-mile stretch of the *Westwall* between Bleialf and Sevenig. To the south of Hodges, Patton's Third Army was a mere seventeen miles from the German frontier and on Patton's southern flank Patch's Seventh Army was catching up fast. Why wasn't

---

* Other titles include *A Bridge at Arnhem, Operation Northwind, The Last Assault* and *Siegfried: the Nazis' Last Stand*, mostly published by Leo Cooper Ltd.

a decisive thrust, using all available strength, made that September? It would undoubtedly have brought the war in the West to a speedy end.

Fifty years ago that question could only have been answered by one man. He was the Allied Supreme Commander, General Eisenhower. Eleven days before the first Americans of the 5th Armored Division penetrated the Siegfried Line, Eisenhower had taken over the command of all Allied ground forces from General Montgomery. It had been his boss in Washington, the austere General Marshall, who wouldn't even let the President of the United States call him by his first name, who had suggested that he should do so.

Today we can only conjecture why Marshall made the suggestion. After all, throughout his thirty-year Army career, Eisenhower had never commanded troops in action. In essence Eisenhower was a chair-borne general, who combined military skill with diplomacy. His strategic ideas were limited and Marshall knew it. So why did he make the suggestion?

The fact that it was election year in the United States might have influenced Marshall. Victory in Europe might well mean re-election for President Roosevelt, but that victory had to be achieved by an *American* ground force commander, not a British one. Besides, for every British soldier serving under Eisenhower there were now *three* American ones.

Indeed that autumn it seemed as if the American Top Brass were determined that they, and they only, would gain the kudos for victory in Europe. The winning of the war would be an exclusively American affair, regardless of the strategies planned before the campaign had begun. As Patton summed it up one night to his old comrade 'Big Simp' Simpson, the commander of the US 9th Army: 'Well, here we all are under Eisenhower and Bradley, both six years our junior. Hodges flunked out of West Point. Now he commands First Army. I was turned back from '08 [the class of that year] and it took me five years to grad-uate. But now I command Third Army. You came second from the bottom in our class in '09 and now you command Ninth Army. Isn't it odd that three old farts like us should be carrying the ball for those two sons-of-bitches?'

It was this strong bond based on the common alma mater, West Point – a kind of old boy network shared by Eisenhower, Bradley and Ike's three army commanders – that became the critical factor in determining the conduct of the war that autumn. Each of them wanted to ensure that it was an *American* general who won the war in the West. Not only did they refuse to give support to 'that little Limey fart' Montgomery up in the north, who was best placed for a decisive breakthrough into the Reich, but they also competed against each other. Every one of them wanted to achieve personal glory – and damn the rest!

In the end it was America's 'Forgotten Army', the Seventh, which reached the Rhine first, four months before Hodges' First Army made the impromptu and unplanned crossing of the river at Remagen in March 1945.* Devers, commanding the US 6th Army Group, to which the Seventh Army belonged, at once ordered patrols across the Rhine, who reported back that the bunkers of the Siegfried Line on the other side were unmanned and there was no sign of the enemy. The River Rhine was ripe for the taking.

Two days after the Rhine had been reached, Eisenhower, in a foul temper, and Bradley journeyed south to meet Devers. Eisenhower, who disliked Devers, as did Bradley, and would have fired him if he had been able to, ordered that all planning to cross the Rhine in corps strength had to cease *immediately*. Instead the Seventh would first mop up the west bank and then turn and support Patton in the Saar basin. Even though Patton was delighted by the news, he did confide to his diary that day that 'I personally believe that VI Corps (of the Seventh Army) should have crossed the Rhine, but it was stopped by Eisenhower the day he visited Devers.' Devers protested against the decision vigorously in a late night meeting which went on to the small hours of the following morning. But Eisenhower overruled him. Devers noted later in his diary, 'I feel as if I don't belong to the same team.'

'It is interesting to conjecture,' Patch's chief engineer, General Garrison H. Davidson, recalled thirty years later, 'what might have been the effect of the exploitation of the unexpected crossing of the Rhine in late November or early December and envelopment of the Ruhr – what might have happened had Ike had the audacity to take a calculated risk as Patton would have, instead of playing it safe.'

But Eisenhower didn't take that calculated risk. Devers was well and truly stopped. The kudos of being the first American army to cross the Rhine would be gained by one of Eisenhower's inner circle, Hodges' First. Devers' Seventh would stay on the Rhine for another four months and would be the last to cross on 26 March, 1945.

So the long 350-mile front bogged down again. From the top there

---

* It is indicative of how the Seventh Army has been neglected by US historians that the official history of its campaign in France and Germany was only published in 1993, decades after the accounts of Hodges' and Patton's armies.

seemed no direction. November gave way to December. An irate Montgomery complained on 16 December to SHAEF's Chief-of-Operations, General Sir John Whiteley, that, unless the Supreme Commander made up his mind soon about what he wanted to do and gave definite orders, the Allies were likely 'to drift into an unfavourable situation vis-à-vis the enemy'.

They were prophetic words. On that same Saturday morning 200,000 German troops launched a counter-attack in the Ardennes against US General Middleton's 80,000 strong VIII Corps. The Battle of the Bulge had started.

★   ★   ★

Three months later, on the dawn of Tuesday, 20 March, 1945, the 70th Division's artillery opened up. The first American shells zipped over the heads of the infantry waiting in their foxholes and slammed into the German positions on the other side of the River Saar. The assault barrage had begun. Above the racket NCOs yelled, 'OK. Let's go!'

The infantry rose apprehensively. Bodies crouched, they moved forward in ragged lines. Any moment now they knew the Krauts would open up. The bitter killing game they had been forced to play these last three months since they had first arrived in France would start again. They came ever closer to the bunkers. In the incandescent light cast by the bursting phosphorous shells they could see the German wire with the squat concrete bunkers beyond quite clearly. Why hadn't the defenders opened up yet? Out there in the open they were sitting ducks.

Now the men of the first wave were scrambling over the rusting wire. This was the signal for the US artillery to cease firing. The shelling stopped. The infantry hesitated. The officers barked, 'Keep moving!'

But the attack was faltering. Not because of the enemy. The faces of the infantrymen reflected their sudden surprise. *The German bunkers were empty!* The enemy had done a bunk. They had abandoned their Siegfried Line positions during the hours of darkness. The last stretch of the Great Wall of Germany had been finally broken. The Siegfried Line on which the Tommies had been going to hang out their washing so long before had fallen at last.

In the years to come, Colonel Cheves, a battalion commander much respected by his troops because they knew he wouldn't squander their lives needlessly, would often wonder why it had taken so long to break through the Siegfried line – from 11 September, 1944, until 20 March, 1945. It was a question that often troubled him. Why had so many lives been sacrificed? What had gone wrong?

Death on a Distant Frontier is an attempt to answer those questions.

Bleialf, Germany/York, England, Winter 1995.

I

SEPTEMBER-OCTOBER, 1944

'Maybe there are five thousand, maybe ten thousand Nazi bastards in their concrete foxholes before the Third Army. Now if Ike stops holding Monty's hand and gives me the supplies, *I'll go through the Siegfried Line like shit through a goose!*'

General Patton, September, 1944.

1

AIRBORNE SPEARHEAD

The soldiers who would drop into enemy territory this night had all been kitted out. By 1944 the informal dress they had worn in the desert had been replaced by standard British battledress, parachute helmet and rubber-soled boots. All were heavily armed, with a scabbard strapped to the right leg, while on the left there was tied a rope to which a 100 lb kitbag would be attached just before they dropped.

Colonel Brian Franks, their commander, a veteran of the war in the shadows in North Africa, Sicily and Italy, nodded his approval. Most of the men who would jump with him this September night had never taken part in ops before, but they were remarkably calm, getting on with the job with no apparent sign of nerves, not much different from the handful of veterans he would take with him.

They filed out in the moonlit night and waddled – they all carried sixty pound packs in addition to all the other gear – to the specially converted Halifax bomber of the Royal Air Force's 161st Special Duties Squadron. The pilot saluted Franks, told him and the rest the length of the flight, weather conditions and what they might expect from the enemy. Then they were clambering awkwardly into the four-engined bomber.

The interior was bare and cheerless. There were no seats, only sacks and sleeping bags on the floor, and a bucket. 'Piss bucket,' the sergeant dispatcher told them cheerfully, 'first man to use it empties it afterwards.' Thereupon he started handing out flasks of tea and coffee and packets of 'wads', thick sandwiches of corned beef and hard cheese, standard British Army fare on ops like these.

Under Colonel Franks' supervision, the young troopers lay down on the floor, while the former returned the salute of the base commander, glimpsed outside on the tarmac. It was a tradition in the Special Duties Squadron that these daring young men who might be dead before the night was out had to be honoured by the presence of the airfield's highest-ranking officer.

The lights inside the fuselage went out. The bomber trembled as the pilot ran his four engines at full power. Satisfied that all four were running sweetly, he eased the throttles forward. The Halifax started to rumble down the runway. The last of the flare-path lights loomed up to left and right. The pilot pulled back the stick and they were airborne. Slowly the pilot started to circle in order to gain height.

Franks, sitting with his back to the metal fuselage, could feel it getting colder and colder. But he didn't snuggle beneath the blankets and sacks as his young troopers had already done. Good soldiers that they were, they knew they'd need all the sleep they could get before the 'fun and games' began. Franks's mind was too full of the mission to come.

His task was to lead his unit, the 2nd SAS (the Americans who occasionally served with them called them in a good-natured fashion 'the Sad Athletic Sacks'), into action behind the German lines in France's High Vosges Mountains, some sixty miles from the old French border with the Third Reich. Here he was to blaze a path to the border for the American Seventh Army, commanded by General Patch, coming up from the south, and General Patton's Third Army advancing from the west.

Franks was to do it with small raiding parties of four men in an armoured jeep, who would ambush enemy convoys, destroy German fuel and ammunition dumps and pin-point key targets for the bombers of the RAF. In addition he was to organize and train the local Maquis partisans into a fighting force which could effectively help the Yanks when they came into the mountains.

Now, as he squatted there listening to the soporific drone of the Halifax's engines as the plane headed out over the English Channel, he reflected on those French resistance fighters of all types and political convictions. He knew, of course, that they had done some good work since D-Day eighty-four days before. But dark rumours had been flooding back to Franks's base at Wivenhoe near Colchester that all was not well with the French Maquis. There had been unpleasant tales of informers and traitors, even gangsters, in their ranks; of treachery and counter-treachery, of old scores being settled, even of downright murder.

In the years after the war when Brian Franks helped to re-form the disbanded Special Air Service, he never spoke much about the ill-fated 'Operation Leyton' as this mission was code-named. But at a late hour

4

in the SAS drill hall in London's Duke Street, after much liquor had been consumed, he would sometimes shake his head sadly when he recalled that night of 1/2 September, 1944, and say, '*God, I wish we had never gone.*'

⋆   ⋆   ⋆

In the second half of May, 1944, the 1st SAS Brigade had been sealed up in their pre-invasion camp at Fairford in Gloucestershire. The régime was strict. In the 'cage', as it became known to the troopers with the winged dagger of the SAS and the motto of 'Who Dares Wins' on their maroon berets, it was ordered that no one was to leave on pain of years in the 'glasshouse'.⋆ Sentries were posted outside to see that they didn't.

But, despite all the warnings and restrictions, one member of the SAS Brigade had kept disappearing from the 'cage' – some said twelve times in all – to reappear a few days later looking tired but thoughtful. He was the commanding officer of the 1st SAS Regiment, Colonel Blair Mayne, known to his men simply as 'Colonel Paddy'. The massive Irishman (6ft 5ins and broad with it) was a sandy-haired, softly spoken ex-solicitor who had played international rugby and boxed as a heavyweight for his native country. But if Colonel Paddy was softly spoken, he did have a hair-trigger temper. That temper, indeed, had first brought him to the SAS back in 1941 in Egypt just after the Special Air Service had been formed by the future Colonel David Stirling.

In the 11th Scottish Commando, with which Mayne had been serving at the time, he had formed a strong dislike for his 24-year-old Commanding Officer, Lieutenant-Colonel Geoffrey Keyes, who would soon win a posthumous Victoria Cross for his attempt to capture or kill Field Marshal Rommel. Once he had chased his C.O. out of the mess with a drawn bayonet. Then he committed the ultimate military sin. He struck his Commanding Officer!

Thus it was that Mayne was languishing in a Cairo Military Prison, awaiting his court-martial, which would probably have resulted with his being cashiered, when a friend arranged for him to be brought under an armed escort to meet Stirling, with a view to perhaps joining the newly formed SAS.

As Stirling described that meeting many years later, 'He was suspicious of me from the start. We were the same age except for a few months, but here was a man who had seen his fair share of battle and come out

---

⋆British Army prison.

5

of it well. I probably seemed to him as a young whippersnapper who could well have been out to impress the brass.'

The two men discussed the new unorthodox outfit, then, after questioning Stirling in 'rapid-fire style', he said, 'I can't see any prospect of real fighting in this scheme of yours.'

Stirling answered, 'There isn't any. Except against the enemy.'

Mayne laughed and said, 'All right. If you can get me out of here, I'll come along.' He extended a huge paw.

Stirling ignored the proferred handshake. Instead he said, 'There's one more thing. *This* is one commanding officer you never hit and I want you to promise that.' Thereupon he reached out his own hand.

Mayne's face cracked into a smile and he said, 'You have it.' The legendary 'Paddy' Mayne had joined the SAS.

From earlier, unauthorized, jumps into Occupied France to meet and assess the Maquis, Paddy Mayne gained the impression that many of the French Resistance were not to be trusted. He knew that many were brave men and women who were risking their lives for the cause of liberty, but he also discovered that there was suicidal feuding inside the movement. He learned, too, that many agents who had been flown in from Britain to aid the Maquis had been betrayed to the Gestapo for personal reasons, because they didn't belong to the right party (communist) or simply for money. In short Colonel Mayne didn't altogether trust the French Resistance which he was supposed to train and aid. Soon he would find out that his distrust had been well justified.

Throughout June, while the Allies tried to break out of the Normandy beachhead, the 1st SAS Brigade, aided by the Maquis fought desperately to disrupt German communications and prevent them from bringing up reinforcements to attack the beachheads, generally sabotaging German attempts to throw the invaders back into the sea. They penetrated Paris long before Leclerc's 2nd Armoured Division of Patton's Third Army. They discovered Rommel's HQ and were planning to 'kill or kidnap him' (as their orders read) just before he was seriously wounded by an RAF fighter-bomber. Indeed one of their sub-units, the Belgian SAS, operating out of the Ardennes forest in their own country, actually penetrated Germany itself before beating a hasty and successful retreat! Within days of the D-Day landings this small force of very brave men, working in jeep teams of four troopers, were operating behind German lines, from Brittany on the French coast to the Vosges Mountains in Alsace. 2,500 men, operating against massive German superiority (in one case a handful of SAS troopers, supported by local Maquisards, had 'persuaded' 1,300 German soldiers led by a full general to surrender to the Americans at Issoudon) were operating from forty-three separate bases.

June gave way to July and the Allies had still not broken out of their Normandy beachheads, Colonel Paddy Mayne's fears of French treachery were finally realized.

*   *   *

Throughout that June his 'B' Squadron, led by 23-year-old Captain John Tonkin, who had already escaped from probable execution by jumping out of a German troop train in Italy, had been blowing up bridges and rolling stock in the general area of Poitiers in an attempt to help Patch's 7th US Army coming up from the south. On 27 June, however, two of his troopers were captured trying to destroy some marshalling yards in the area held by the German 80th Corps, made up of German reserve units, Russian Cossacks and the 950th Indian Regiment.* The two SAS prisoners refused to give their interrogators any information, but it was established that they belonged to the SAS. Immediately General Gallenkamp, commanding 80 Corps, ordered these 'saboteurs and bandits' to be found. The hunt for Tonkin's 'B' Squadron was on.

On the afternoon of 1 July Trooper John Fielding was on guard at the forest camp of the SAS 'when I saw a motorcycle and sidecar being pushed down the incline towards me, along the road, by two *maquis* with black berets. They arrived at the track and I laid low for a few minutes. I then showed myself and started talking to them. They explained to me that they had got a puncture in the wheel of the sidecar and after consideration I took them up the track to the base where John Tonkin saw them and the necessary repairs were carried out. They spent some time at the base.'

After explaining to the local Maquis at Tonkin's forest hideout that they belonged to another outfit, they were allowed to leave. Naturally both Frenchmen were spies for the Germans. Now that the enemy knew where the SAS were located, they acted promptly. A force of Gestapo, 400 SS from a training unit and a cycle reconnaissance company under the command of *Oberleutnant* Vogt, a former Protestant pastor, was formed. It would have the task of launching a surprise attack on Tonkin's Company and their Maquis helpers.

---

* Renegade soldiers of the British Indian Army, who, after being taken prisoner by the Germans, had gone over to them and joined the 'Indian Legion' (*Freies Indien*).

They attacked at dawn on Monday, 3 July. The outposts were attacked first as the SS men came through the trees firing Schmeissers from the hip. Then their mortars joined in.

Immediately alert, John Tonkin considered what he was to do. Firing seemed to be coming from all sides. Now he could see Germans in camouflaged tunics working along the hedgerows some 200 yards off. For a few moments he considered fighting it out with the help of the three Vickers machine guns mounted on the squadron's jeeps. But he decided against it. There were two many attackers. He went back to his men and told them they'd use their standard operating procedure in situations like this. They would scatter in ones and twos through the trees and make for the large forest to the west where they would lie low.

But it wasn't to be. Suddenly a half-naked SAS trooper panicked. He ran through the group crying at the top of his voice, '*They're coming! They're coming!*'

His panic was infectious. A large group of Maquisards and SAS troopers started to run down the slope into the valley below. Tonkin knew that this was the worst thing they could have done. He yelled at them to stand fast, but no one heeded him.

So he concentrated on the men who had not panicked and began dispatching them in couples towards the large forest to the west. Suddenly he remembered that their transmitter and the vital, top secret Sabu 4 code book had been left behind and doubled back to get it. Too late! He saw the Germans coming in on both flanks. He was cut off.

Professional as ever, he went to ground. 'I sat down in some rough ground a little way down the slope and about 50 yards from the camp. The cover was very thin.' Pulling up his camouflaged jacket to hide his face, he froze. Just in time. A German carrying a Schmeisser appeared just above on the top of the slope and peered into the valley, but he didn't see the concealed officer. He went away and, breathing a sigh of relief, Tonkin stole into the forest. Behind him heavy machine guns opened up as the SS swept the trees with tracer, trying to flush out the party that had fled in panic. Captain Tonkin would never see them again alive.

⋆　　⋆　　⋆

They shot the thirty SAS prisoners and one American who was with them on the morning of 7 July, 1944. The firing squad was made up of men from the cycle reconnaissance company, commanded by the former pastor, Vogt. The condemned men gave their watches and other personal effects to them for 'safe keeping', as the Germans explained after the war.

Most of them were teenagers under a 'senior officer', Lieutenant Crisp, all of 20, who had been wounded himself when he had stayed behind in the forest to tend a seriously wounded trooper. But, as one German observer reported after the war, 'The execution was accomplished militarily and with dignity. The parachutists died in an exemplary, brave and calm manner. After the decision of the execution had been made known to them in the English language by an interpreter, the prisoners – they were not chained – stood in line. They linked arms. The fire order was given by *Oberleutnant* Vogt.'

Reporting the execution to General Gallenkamp, commander of the German 80th Corps, the officer concerned said, 'General, you may be assured that this was the most terrible day and the hardest hour of my life.' It was said that the reporting officer's eyes filled with tears at that moment.

Vogt, who gave the firing squad the order to fire, apparently showed no emotion. After all, as they said in the German Army, '*Befehl ist Befehl*' (Orders are orders).*

★   ★   ★

On the same day that the SAS troopers were shot nine men of Paddy Mayne's 'D' Squadron were being tortured at Gestapo HQ in the Avenue Foch in Paris. Three of them, including the Squadron Commander, Captain Garstin, were wounded and in a pitiful state from lack of blood.

Pat Garstin's men had dropped at a site personally selected by Mayne in the great Forest of Fontainebleau not far from where the Supreme Commander, General Eisenhower, would have his HQ outside Paris. They had been unlucky. The drop had been betrayed by a Maquisard in advance. As they landed they were greeted by a group of men in civilian clothes, who cried, '*Vive la France*'. Next moment the Maquis had opened up with automatic weapons.

After a month of torture by the Gestapo, which failed to break them, the SAS prisoners were told on 8 August by a sergeant major in the SS that they were going to be sent to Switzerland to be exchanged for

* Three of the captured SAS troopers, all in their early twenties, who had been wounded, were shamefully neglected by the German medics. Finally they were put out of their misery by lethal injections given by the German M.O.

German agents being held in London. He said, 'As you are going via Switzerland, which is neutral, you will have to wear civilian clothes.'

The SS man smiled at the prisoners, but they were suspicious until the wounded Captain Garstin reassured them.

At midnight that day the prisoners were led to a truck, guarded by two SS men armed with automatics. One of them spoke French and SAS Corporal Serge Vaculik, a Czech who had been brought up in France, tried to engage him in some friendly conversation. To no avail.

They set off into the night. In the moonlight they could see, by peering through a gap in the canvas, that they were being followed by two carloads of SS men. Now the prisoners started to get worried. Why waste precious petrol on two carloads of SS men to guard them? They weren't going to escape if they were about to be exchanged. Again Vaculik tackled the French-speaking SS man. Were they really going to Switzerland? Gruffly he was told to shut up. They'd learn soon enough where they were heading for.

They did. A little later the little convoy turned off the main road and headed across a field for two hundred yards or so, bumping up and down over the rough pasture. Now the prisoners were afraid. This wasn't planned. What were the SS up to?

The truck stopped. The prisoners were ordered out as the SS spilled out from their cars, pistols already in their hands. Alarmed, Vaculik turned to the guard who spoke French. 'Are we going to be shot?' he demanded.

The guard laughed. 'Of course you're going to be shot. What did you think this was – a *picnic*?'

Garstin reacted promptly. He whispered to Corporal 'Ginger' Jones to his right, 'When I say now, run for it.' He told Vaculik the same. The men whispered the instruction to the rest of the prisoners.

A Gestapo man posted himself in front of the SAS troopers. He read something in German from a paper. None of them could understand him. It didn't matter. They were tensing for the breakout. A sergeant took the paper from the civilian and began to read in English, 'For having wished to work in collaboration with the French terrorists and thus to endanger the security of the German Army you are condemned to the penalty of death and shall be shot.'

'*SHOT*' triggered the breakout.

'*NOW!*' Garstin bellowed.

They all ran for it save Captain Garstin who was still in bad shape from his wound. The SS opened up at once. Bullets sliced the air. Five men went down at once. Captain Garstin was shot where he stood. But Corporal Vaculik and Corporal Jones managed to dodge the slugs. They pelted across the field, arms working like pistons, heading for the woods beyond. And they made it.

For a few days the two fugitives hid in the village of Hermas until the Americans, advancing on Paris, finally liberated the place. Thus it was that on 28 August they were back at Mayne's HQ, relating what had happened to the men of 'D' Squadron, while Colonel Paddy listened in silence.

★   ★   ★

Now, as Colonel Franks prepared to drop, he knew from his friend Blair Mayne that, through betrayal by their supposed allies, the 1st SAS had paid a terrible price for helping to spearhead the attack of the two American armies marching eastwards. Would his own 2nd SAS Regiment, soon to go into action in the Vosges, be betrayed too?

But there was no time to think about the future now. The sergeant-dispatcher had warned them they were approaching the DZ. They had a last drink from their flasks. They strapped the 100lb kitbags to the quick-release clips below their knees. Franks positioned himself at the jump hole on the Halifax's floor. Below in the moonlight he could see the dark fields passing by. To the west he glimpsed a small collection of other houses. That would be Veney close to the DZ. The reception party was coming from the village, he knew. The dispatcher raised his right arm. The red warning light changed to green. 'Go!' the RAF sergeant yelled above the roar of the engines. Colonel Franks pushed himself into space. They were on their way.

2

BETRAYAL

Five hours after the SAS had landed with three casualties on that morning of 2 September the commander of the army they had come to help received an urgent phonecall. General Patton, at his HQ at Châlons, was summoned immediately to a meeting of the top US brass at the headquarters of his chief, Bradley, in Chartres some 130 miles away. He was expected to be there by eleven o'clock when Eisenhower would arrive. But the weather was too bad to fly, so Patton would have to go by car and at top speed.

The order put Patton in a bad mood, not made any better by the thought of the way Ike had praised Montgomery on the occasion of Ike's take-over of the command of all Allied land forces the previous day. Knowing that Montgomery, who had previously held that post, had been criticized for his slowness in breaking out of the beachhead, Eisenhower had told the world press, that 'anyone who interprets this [the command change-over] as a demotion for General Montgomery won't look facts in the face. He is not only my very close and warm friend [but] one of the great soldiers of this or any other war.'

The fact that Eisenhower had praised the 'little fart' (as Patton called Montgomery) so fulsomely rankled, especially since Ike had not seen fit to visit his Third Army for three months. Nor was Patton's mood made any better by the fact that, though his driver was going all out, they were running very late. Indeed it was 12.45 when he spotted the spires of Chartres cathedral. He was nearly two hours late for his meeting with the Supreme Commander.

All the same Patton thought that congratulations were in order. Ike, he felt, ought to praise the Third Army, and naturally Patton, for the speed with which it had broken out of the beachhead and reached the River Meuse in such a short time.

But Eisenhower was strictly business. The usual grin was absent as he shook hands with Patton, who thought it was something to do with his tardiness. In fact Eisenhower was angry, very angry, with Patton because, as his secretary-cum-mistress, the ex-British model Kay Summersby noted in her diary for that day: 'Eisenhower says he is going to give Patton hell because he is stretching the line too far and therefore making supply difficulties.'

The conference began. Eisenhower pontificated at length about Clausewitz, the great 19th century Prussian military philosopher. Patton's anger grew. Clausewitz had commanded forces that weren't armoured and numbered only a quarter of the 450,000 men that he now commanded.

Eisenhower droned about the future 'great battle of Germany'. Listening impatiently, Patton thought, 'If we wait, there *will* be a great battle of Germany.' He decided it was time to play his hand. He rose and said in his high-pitched, squeaky voice, 'We have patrols on the Moselle near Nancy, Ike.' This was stretching the facts a little, for his 35th Infantry Division was still miles away from the Lorraine capital. Then Patton, in his eagerness to obtain concessions from Eisenhower for his Third Army, stretched the truth even further. He said, 'Patrols of my 3rd Cavalry have actually entered Metz!'

That made some of the brass sit up. If Patton had men in Metz already, the German frontier was only a day's march away. In fact, Patton's Army was stalled just outside Verdun, some twenty-five miles from Metz. Indeed it would take Patton nearly *three months* to conquer Metz.

But Patton pressed home his advantage. 'If you let me retain my regular tonnage, we could push on to the German frontier and rupture that goddam Siegfried Line.' Only the day before he had boasted to his admiring staff that if he 'got the green light I could go through the Siegfried Line like shit through a goose!' So he added confidently, 'I'm willing to stake my reputation on that.'

'Careful, George,' Eisenhower said somewhat wearily, 'that reputation of yours hasn't been worth very much.' The Supreme Commander was referring to a string of incidents dating back to the slapping of the soldier suffering from combat fatigue in Sicily in 1943, which had resulted in very bad publicity back in the States and demands for Patton's dismissal.

Eisenhower said the words with a disarming smile, but they hurt Patton. Then he remembered the first batch of newspaper clippings he had received two days before from the States, praising his Third Army and his leadership. From them he had concluded that all was forgiven back home. So, hiding his irritation at Ike's remark, he hitched up his belt, with the two famous pistols attached to it, and said quietly, 'That reputation is pretty good now'.

The conference continued. The new Land Commander gave his approval to Bradley continuing his drive to the east, in particular Patton's Third Army, aided by General Gerow's Vth Corps from Hodges' First Army on Patton's left flank. But Eisenhower qualified his assent. He said, 'We have advanced so rapidly that further movement in large parts of the front, even against very weak opposition, is almost impossible. The closer we get to the Siegfried Line, the more we will be stretched administratively and eventually a period of inaction will be imposed upon us. The potential danger is that while we are temporarily stalled the enemy will be able to pick up bits and pieces of forces everywhere and organize them swiftly for defending the Siegfried Line on the Rhine. It is obvious from an overall point of view that we must now, as never before, keep the enemy stretched everywhere.'

Try as they may, Patton and Bradley could not convince Eisenhower to change his intentions; one could hardly call them plans. 'We have an excellent plan,' Patton persisted, 'for a drive through the Nancy Epinal gap. The Siegfried Line is not manned yet, and the Huns have little if anything in the area to stop us. If you let me go and give me what we need, we can be in Germany at the Rhine in ten days!'

Eisenhower remained adamant. Neither Montgomery's plan to drive to the Ruhr and then on to Berlin nor Patton's to attack through the Siegfried Line for the Rhine would work. The key to the whole of the future battle of Germany was supplies. Till the supply situation to the rear was cleared up, *all* his armies would advance the best they could on what was later called the Broad Front Strategy to the German frontier. That was that!

★   ★   ★

It was the unforgiving moment. Eisenhower's decision on that gloomy Saturday afternoon meant that three giant army groups, Montgomery's 21st, Bradley's 12th and Devers' 6th, would lumber ponderously towards the German frontier, with not one of them singly powerful enough to break through the Siegfried Line. Ever afterwards Patton and Bradley would blame Montgomery, maintaining that Eisenhower favoured him with unfair shares of the supplies available. Indeed Patton grew to believe that Eisenhower was actively sabotaging the amount of supplies that should have been coming his way. Montgomery, for his part, thought that all the American top brass, including Eisenhower, were at fault for not letting him get on with a forty-division thrust to the Ruhr. In fact the fault was Eisenhower's. In that first week of September, when the German Army was in retreat and totally disorganized, either Patton or Montgomery could have gone through the Siegfried Line like Patton's proverbial goose, given the necessary numbers and supplies.

But that wasn't to be. That day, as Eisenhower flew back to his headquarters at Granville on the French coast, he had made a decision which would result in two-thirds of all the casualties to be suffered in the campaign in Europe. The war would drag on for another nine months. It would take six of those months alone to break through the Siegfried Line. Now division after division would be thrown at the *Westwall*. Death on a distant frontier would now be the fate of thousands upon thousands of young Allied soldiers. Perhaps unwittingly, the Supreme Commander had established the greatest killing zone in North-West Europe.

★　★　★

So while Patton fumed impotently, his soldiers took time out of battle to enjoy themselves. For most of his fighting soldiers, their lives were short and brutal. Now, after six weeks of almost constant combat, they need a diversion. Although the German *Luftwaffe* were bombing the US 7th Armored Division's bridgehead at Verdun, Lieutenant Will Rogers Jr decided to take his platoon on a tour of the historic First World War battlefield on the heights above the city. He had been there before as a child with his father, the famous American humorist Will Rogers.

The young officer, who had resigned from Congress in order to get into combat showed them the memorial to a certain Sergeant Maginot who had lost a leg in the famous battle of 1916 and had sworn that France would never be invaded again, hence that celebrated white elephant, the Maginot Line, which Patton's Third Army would soon be attacking. Rogers explained to his men the 'Trench of Bayonets' where the rusting bayonets of a French infantry company buried alive in a sudden German bombardment still poked through the earth. But just as he was about to explain how the Germans had attacked that year, the voice of the task force commander of the 814 Tank Destroyer Battalion came over the radio, interrupting the history lesson, with 'Lieutenant Rogers, *please*, let's fight one war at a time!'

Not far away an infantryman of the 5th Infantry Division, which soon would be battling with the 7th Armored to cross the River Moselle, chalked on the wall of the fortress of Verdun: '*Austin White – Chicago, Ill – 1918. Austin White – Chicago, Ill, 1944* and then added, '*This is the last time I want to write my name here.*'

The divisions which would attack across the Moselle and into the Siegfried Line waited for the new battle to begin. The men of the nine divisions under Patton's command slept the clock round, ate fresh food, obtained by barter rather than the canned rations they had been living off since 1 August, 1944, got a little drunk and, if they were very lucky, got laid. Their mood was buoyant. The war seemed about over bar the shouting. The enemy was in full retreat. One last push, they told themselves, and it would be all over.

For his part, Patton went sight-seeing over the countryside where he had fought back in 1918. 'This is where we came in,' he told his aide, Colonel Codman, like himself a veteran of the First World War. Old mistresses were looked up. The place where he had been wounded twenty-six years before was rediscovered. As Codman remarked, 'He has a great deal of sentiment about World War One.'

All the same Patton fumed at the forced inactivity, blaming it all on Montgomery, who had been appointed a British Field Marshal on the first day of September in way of compensation for losing his overall command of Allied land forces.

At one meeting with newspaper correspondents in that first week of September, after attacking the 'Holy Monk', the religiously inclined General Lee, commander of Com-Z⋆, he turned his attention to Montgomery, 'Yesterday the *Field Marshal*,' he emphasized the rank contemptuously, 'ordered SHAEF to have Third Army go on the defensive, stand in place and prepare to guard his right flank. The Field Marshal then announced that he will, after regrouping, make what he describes as a lightning dagger-thrust at the heart of Germany. "They will be off their guard," the Field Marshal predicts, "and I shall pop out at them – *like an angry rabbit!*"'

On 5 September Bradley arrived at Patton's HQ in Châlons-sûr-Marne bearing glad tidings. He told Patton that he had the green light. He could start advancing again and he would be adequately supplied with petrol. Patton was delighted. He summoned his three corps comman-

⋆ The US rearline supply organisation

ders and outlined what he expected them to do: a hasty plan, if it could be called a plan, which later became Field Order No.10.

It was a superbly optimistic plan. It stated that 'Third US Army attacks to seize crossings of the Rhine River between Mannheim and Coblenz.'

Naturally there were a few obstacles in the way. There was the River Moselle for example. That would be the job of Walker's XX Corps. Once the fat general with the bulldog face had crossed with his Seventh Armored Division, his Fifth Infantry would tackle Metz, another unknown quality, for Patton knew little of the defences along the Moselle and nothing about those in Metz, which had not been taken from the east since the 5th century.

Meanwhile Walker's 90th Division would capture Thionville to the north of Metz. With the Moselle line broken through at a length of some twenty miles, the 3rd Army's 3rd Cavalry Group was to 'reconnoiter to the Rhine without delay' and the 7th Armored Division was to 'advance east in multiple columns to seize crossings over the Rhine.' Cities and strongpoints were to be by-passed and left to be mopped up by the following infantry.

Field Order No.10 was truly a masterpiece of strategic planning, but far too vague and based on so many imponderables. In ten days, as he had promised Eisenhower it would take to reach the Rhine, Patton intended to breach the Moselle, capture one of the most fortified cities in Europe, break through the Siegfried Line and advance across the rugged Eifel Mountains, with few good roads for armour, to the Rhine. All this with little hard intelligence about the enemy's defences and intentions. Indeed Patton's Third Army had run out of military maps and were using Michelin road maps of the 1:100,000 type!

All this didn't seem to bother Patton in his search for glory and a place in American military history. As he had written to himself when a youth, fascinated with the Pattons' historic and heroic past: 'Remember you have placed all on war. Therefore you must never fail . . . If you do not die a soldier and having had a chance to be one, I pray God to damn you George Patton . . . Never, never, never stop being ambitious. You have but one life. Live it to the full of glory and be willing to pay.' Now Patton would have the glory. His soldiers would do the paying.

★   ★   ★

Colonel Franks and his 2nd SAS were betrayed right from the start. That morning, as they had come floating down to the DZ at three o'clock, lit by domestic flashlights, the firing had begun at once. Gaston Fouche, one of the welcoming party of Colonel Maximum's Maquis, had opened fire on them with his Sten gun. He was suspected of being in German pay. Now Captain Druce of the SAS's advance party, dropped two weeks before, raced up to him. He had already experienced betrayal at the hands of the Maquis and he was in no mood to trifle. He grabbed Fouche and shot him dead through the heart.

Swiftly Druce filled his Colonel in as all around the Maquis shouted noisily in French and Russian. There were Russian deserters from the *Wehrmacht* among Colonel Maximum's ranks. His news wasn't good. Maximum's Maquis were untrained, indiscreet and noisy. It seemed, too, that their ranks were riddled with traitors.

Franks made a snap decision. He would operate without the Maquis and he would keep his hideouts hidden from both the Germans and the Maquis. So the little band of SAS troopers in their armoured jeeps set off to conduct their war in the shadows, preparing the way for the two US armies marching east. Behind them they left in hiding the three men who had been injured in the drop, Sergeant Fitzpatrick, Privates Elliott and Conway, not one of them over 21. They lay low in a wood near a remote farm. But not for long. They were betrayed to the local Gestapo by a woman, Genevieve Demetz. In due course, they were tortured, shot and their bodies burned outside the farm.

Fighting both their anger at these 'saboteurs and gangsters' in their midst and the ever-present threat that the French would betray them, Franks and his eighty-odd troopers kept up a running battle with the enemy. They killed enemy soldiers, blew up enemy vehicles, destroyed railways and railway lines. Once they entered the hamlet of La Chapelotte to be confronted by a hugely superior German force. Franks's men didn't hesitate. There was a shoot-out at point blank range and then, obeying the SAS's dictum of 'shoot and scoot', they scooted.

Erich Marcks, living in a hamlet just outside the village of Wingen, a handful of miles from the old German frontier, remembers being called out by the local Gestapo man to hunt 'enemy soldiers who had landed by parachute'. Armed with a hunting rifle, the 16-year-old advanced through a cornfield with his fellow members of the Hitler Youth.

'Suddenly a man in a red beret popped up out of the corn to our front. The Gestapo *Kommissar* said, "Shoot!" That didn't frighten the man in the beret. Perhaps he didn't understand because the order was given in German. In French, the man in the red beret said very calmly, "I think it's better if you and your boys should go home while you're still safe."'

The fat Gestapo man looked as if he might explode, but he knew his own life was on the line. As the man in the red beret ducked back into cover, he said, 'All right boys, let's go home to mother'.

Fifty years on, Erich, now an old man, could grin at the memory of what happened so long ago in the field just outside his home and say, 'Well, I've always been able to say I fought against the English SAS — *and lived.*'

But as the eighty-seven troopers under Franks's command, ranged far and wide in the frontier area, attacking all the time, moving from one secret location to another in the rugged, wooded mountainous area of the Lower Vosges, the Germans believed they were faced with a force much larger than one which amounted to not much more than a company. Two German *divisions* were sent in to deal with them. Though not up to full strength, these Germans were many times the number of the SAS. Pressure began to mount. Franks found that it was becoming ever more difficult to mount an operation and get away safely. The Germans seemed to be everywhere now.

Once he found himself almost trapped. In an attempt to break out, he dispatched a party under a Lieutenant Black to lead the Germans astray. It worked. The main party escaped, but as Black headed for the emergency rendezvous at the Lac de la Maix, he was betrayed to the Gestapo by a Maquisard who had acted as a guide for the SAS, Gaston Matthieu.

The rendezvous was at a sawmill on the lake at La Turbine. Now, as seven SAS troopers approached under Black's command, they became aware of the soft tread of boots in the trees and the fact that the birds had stopped singing. Black was on the alert immediately. He knew what that meant. The Germans were closing in on them. Softly he ordered they should slip away. Too late! The Germans had already spotted them. Ragged gunfire broke out. Black and his party went to ground. For four long hours the eight held off the Germans until Black was wounded in the leg and could move no more and the ammunition of the rest ran out. One by one they were hauled from their hiding places by the Germans and dragged roughly to the truck which would take them to Strasbourg for interrogation by the Gestapo. Not one of them had any illusions what would happen to them. Still, as the Gestapo records found after the war show, none of them betrayed anything of importance. So in the end the frustrated Gestapo men gave up on them and shot them out of hand.*

Franks started to worry. He was losing men too fast. He asked for

---

* Their graves, like those of the other heroes of the SAS, are not far away from where they were shot at Duenbach, Alsace.

assistance and received a paradrop of six armoured jeeps, equipped with twin-barrelled Vickers K machine guns, always a great favourite with the SAS, and twin-barrelled Browning machine guns. Franks threw them into the running battle with the Germans who were now out in full force, trying to clean up their rear areas before the Americans of the US 3rd and 7th Armies attacked towards the frontier.

Captain Druce, who had been fighting and running since 14 August when he had parachuted in with the SAS advance party, was delighted with the new armoured jeeps. Together with a Lieutenant Manners in a second jeep they set off to ambush a German convoy on the Senonnes-Moyenmoutier road. Unknown to the two young officers their mission had been betrayed to the Germans by a French double-agent. As the two jeeps approached the curve in the country road where they intended to set up the ambush, tracer started to zip towards them. Druce reacted correctly at once. He swung the wheel round and went straight into the field to his right. Manners followed suit. Then they were racing away, followed by a hail of fire. They had dodged the trap.

A little later they shot up a car which they thought belonged to the Gestapo. In fact it was owned by a local mayor, Monsieur Pi. The latter was unhurt and later he had a message delivered to the SAS thanking them for the 'salute of honour', which was more than welcome because it was accompanied by two bottles of vintage champagne!

On that same day the four other jeeps joined a German convoy. They succeeded in destroying most of it before more Germans arrived on the scene. Franks, followed by another jeep, took off across country. Again they couldn't escape the Germans who were determined to wipe them out. In the battle which followed, eight men against some eighty SS men, Franks's jeep overturned and the one following ran straight into an ambush. Both jeeps had to be abandoned, but the SAS managed to fight their way out on foot.

But Colonel Franks, who had now suffered fifty percent casualties, was growing weary of the constant fighting and running. The fact that, although there were loyal French people prepared to help him and his men, there were far too many traitors who would betray them to the Germans at the drop of a hat, also depressed him. Time was running out for him and his handful of survivors. Over and over again he kept asking himself, *'Where are the Americans?'*

3

PATTON TAKES A HAND

Now the assault divisions of Patton's Third Army prepared for the attack on the River Moselle. The tanks of the 7th Armored Division which would lead the drive were filled up with precious petrol. Ammunition, though still in short supply (in some cases there were only five shells per gun available), was brought up. The infantry were handed extra bandoliers and given K-rations for forty-eight hours. Ambulances were parked ready in the Lorraine lanes to ply their trade. Further back the surgeons in the field hospitals prepared for the bloody business soon to come. All was the controlled confusion of an army about to attack.

On the evening of Monday 4 September, the eve of the attack, Colonel Snowdon of the 80th's 317th Regiment was killed while on reconnaissance. Ironically he was the nephew of General Lear, a high-powered general from Washington, whom Patton always regarded as 'Eisenhower's spy' in Europe. But it was another spy which excited the men of the 80th Division that evening. About dusk a young woman was spotted near the command post of the 80th's 318th Regiment. She cycled by the place several times, looking curiously at the preparations being made for the battle to come. In the end the Americans arrested her and took her to the bivouac of Colonel Ralph Pearson in a nearby wood. She appeared to be ravenously hungry and had obviously come a long way on her bicycle to inspect the American CP. So, while she was being fed, the suspicious officers did a quick search of her purse. It was found to contain the enormous sum of 45,000 francs! But there was more to come. After her meal she asked for her bag and took out her powder compact. One of the US officers, Frank Hatry, who had lived in Paris before the war, noticed that she was looking for something other than a powder puff in it. He was right. Concealed in the compact there was a code. As Colonel Pearson wrote at the time, 'Things were looking bad for Cecile Henniger.'

In the end, the Colonel gave her his own bedroll and she slept in it that night in the tent under armed guard, while Pearson wondered what to do with her. It wasn't the first time that the 80th Division had come across women working for the Germans. Indeed they had been sniped at by Frenchwomen in their employ and everyone in the division knew someone who knew another G.I. who had actually shot a French woman sniper after capture. But this was the first woman spy the 80th had come across.

On the following morning the worried Colonel, with other things on his mind than women agents, telephoned the US Counter-Intelligence Corps for instructions. The CIC man on the other end of the line reassured him everything was all right. Cecile Henniger *was* an agent but she was working for a friendly power, ie. De Gaulle's France.

For a little while Colonel Pearson pondered the fact that France was spying on the army which had come to liberate the country, but in the end he gave up. But, thereafter, his wife always ribbed him on whether the guards were posted to 'protect *her* from *me* or *me* from *her*'.

*   *   *

The Seventh Armored Division, commanded by General Lindsay Silvester, whom Patton would soon fire because of his handling of the battle, began its attack on the Moselle on 6 September, 1944. Right from the start the going was tough. As soon as the twin columns of armour and mounted infantry rolled along the Verdun-Metz highway the Germans opened up. There were mines everywhere. As soon as the Shermans deployed into the fields they started running into the tank-busting teller mines. It was no better for the infantry. Springing out of their White halftracks to tackle a German strongpoint, they'd step on to the dreaded 'bouncing Betty' anti-personnel mines, which sprang up to waist height, often tearing away some poor GI's manhood, while Spandaus hammered away at them relentlessly.

Still the Seventh Armored pushed on, knowing that their Corps Commander brooked no delay. The bridges across the Moselle were reported all destroyed. Engineers were whistled up to throw Bailey bridges across, once a crossing was secured. But the German defence seemed to grow stronger by the minute. However they tried, the engineers couldn't reach the front, although the men of the 33rd Engineer Battalion went all out. Patton's plan was going badly wrong.

At dawn on the 7th the leading elements of the division, the 23rd Armored Infantry Battalion among them, reached the little riverside village of Dornot. The Germans reacted vigorously. They threw in counter-attack after counter-attack. All the same the Seventh managed to get a patrol across the Moselle where it cowered in German-dug foxholes powerless to contribute anything to the battle. The initiative was obviously passing to the German defenders.

That afternoon General 'Red' Irwin's Fifth Infantry Division, which had been originally intended to 'pin on' to the tail of the Seventh Armored while it drove to the German frontier, was ordered to take over the attack. The Seventh passed into Walker's XX Corps reserve.

'Red' Irwin, a veteran of some of the US Army's earliest battles in North Africa selected his 11th Infantry Regiment to make the crossing at Dornot. He already knew that everything that his men did would be observed from a German fort on a height on the other side. Still he had a chemical warfare company brought up to make a smoke screen which might, hopefully, cover the crossing. So while the US 90th Division covered his left flank and the 80th Division his right, Irwin's 11th Infantry set off to cross the Moselle at 11.15 on the morning of 8 September. They were supported by a tremendous artillery barrage from three entire artillery battalions. And surprisingly enough the first two companies to do so made it with few casualties. But their luck was not going to hold very long.

★   ★   ★

On 8 September Patton was despondent. The men of the 5th Infantry and the Seventh Armored Division's 23rd Armored Infantry Battalion, already across the Moselle, were pinned down; his 90th Division was under attack by the SS of the 17th SS Panzer Grenadier ('Kiss my Arse'★) Division, the young grenadiers penetrating to within fifty yards of the Divisional Commander's CP, while his 80th Division was actually being pushed back.

As always Patton blamed others for his own failings. He told his aide Major Stiller, 'All this comes from the fatal decision of the Supreme Commander to halt the Third Army until the Pas de Calais (ie the supply area) was cleared up.' Naturally Montgomery was behind it all. As Patton stated, 'It is always depressing to me to see how completely Ike is under

---

★ The division's official name was *Goetz von Berchlingen*, a historical figure whom Goethe made to say 'Kiss my arse' in one of his plays.

the influence of the British. He even prefers steel tracks to rubber tracks on tanks because Monty does.'

In the event Patton was almost pathologically anti-British, focusing his hatred on Montgomery, whom he regarded as his rival for Eisenhower's favours. As he remarked in that first week of September, 'We roll across France in less time than it takes Monty to say "regroup" and here we sit stuck in the mud of Lorraine,' adding, '*We* never have to regroup, which seems to be the chief form of amusement for the British Armies.'

Whatever the truth of Patton's comments, it must be remembered that he didn't have much first-hand knowledge of the activities of the British Army, whereas Montgomery had many American units under his command during the campaign, including at times the US 1st and 9th Armies. But Patton never visited the British area of operations. Naturally he knew what Montgomery's 21st Army Group was undertaking, but he never felt the desire to go and see for himself. Indeed he never even visited the US 1st Army on his left flank or the 7th Army on his right because he was jealous of Hodges and of Patch.

Montgomery personally awarded British decorations to American soldiers. He knew most of the American divisional commanders under his command, and often regimental commanders as well. In essence, he saved the US 7th Armored Division during the Battle of the Bulge and he would have probably done the same for the shattered US 106th Infantry Division if he had had the chance.★

But Patton was not interested. He preferred to remain at his Third Army HQ, surrounded by an admiring staff who never contradicted him, all the time feeding his prejudices, reinforcing him in his belief that Eisenhower, Montgomery and other senior officers, British and American, were out to do him down, if not ruin him.

In fact, for the first time in the European campaign Patton had run into serious opposition and he didn't like it. So, as was customary with him, he blamed others for his own failings. If he had been allowed all the petrol he required, he reasoned, then he would have been able to carry out Field Order Number Ten. As he said afterwards, 'I was convinced then [the beginning of September], and have since discovered I was right, that there were no Germans ahead of us except those we were actually fighting. In other words they had no depth.'

★   ★   ★

★ See C. Whiting *The Last Assault*, Leo Cooper, 1994, for further details.

Now the remnants of four German infantry and seven panzer divisions, plus new formations such as the 106th Panzer Brigade, were facing Patton on the Meuse, determined to stop his drive to the Siegfried Line. On the east side of the river the infantry of the 5th and 7th Armored Divisions who had managed to get across were under severe pressure. Between 8 and 10 September the Fifth Division's 11th Infantry fought off *thirty-eight* separate counter-attacks.

Their attackers tried all the tricks of experienced infantry soldiers. Once a German officer managed to make the 11th's 'E' Company stop firing by shouting 'Cease Firing' in English. But the second time he tried he ran out of luck. He and fifteen of his men were mown down.

Another trick used against the American infantry was that employed by two machine gunners working as a pair. One fired tracer at a height of five feet, making the attackers bend low, only to find the second gunner firing non-tracer at two feet. A lot of men went down with leg wounds due to that tricky pair.

On one occasion on the night of 8/9 September German tanks attacked, something tanks normally didn't do at night, followed by infantry shouting *'Yanks kaput!'* The object of the combined infantry-tank attack was obviously to draw American fire so that the defenders' positions would be given away for the usual German dawn attack. The Americans didn't fire, but the many wounded were crying out until 'E' Company's First Sergeant Claude Hembree sent word that the wounded must keep quiet. As the historian of the 11th Infantry Regiment wrote after the war, 'It was accepted by all personnel in the bridgehead that "the wounded don't cry" and they didn't.'

By now Patton had fired the 5th Division's assistant divisional commander, Brigadier-General Thompson, because Patton believed he had abandoned the bridgehead, which he had not. It was just that he couldn't get reinforcements across in the face of withering German fire. The four infantry companies and the thirty-odd men of the Seventh Division's 23rd Armored Infantry Battalion had tried to break out of their positions, but had been forced back into what they called 'Horseshoe Wood', where again they were subjected to bold attacks by fanatical German SS grenadiers. As Captain Gerrie, C.O. of 'G' Company, radioed out of the bridgehead that day, 'Watch out for these birds, they are plenty tough. I've never run across guys like these before. They are new, something you read about.'

But there was plenty of boldness on the American side as well. Private Rex, for instance, who had been in the US Army exactly *eighteen* weeks, took over a machine gun when the gunner was killed. He manned it against Germans attacking with fixed bayonets. He manned it until his ammunition gave out. By then he was surrounded by heaps of dead Germans. Later, during the evacuation, he gave his outer clothing to a wounded man and swam the Meuse four times helping others across.

Up to mid-morning on 9 September it was thought that the bridge-head at Dornot could be held. But then the defenders came under intense fire. As the shells ripped the sky apart and the mortar bombs came hurtling into their slit trenches, the supply of reinforcements for the hard-pressed infantrymen dried up. It was impossible to ferry them across the Meuse. Frantic calls were radioed across the river for air support. But the sky was overcast and it began to rain. Little support was forthcoming.

By now the situation in Horseshoe Wood was steadily becoming worse. Most of the four companies' officers had been killed or wounded. The 11th's 'K' Company was commanded by a sergeant.

Now, because the muzzle flashes betrayed the positions of their only heavy weapons, the 81 mm mortars, the crews had to abandon firing them. Instead they took up and fired the rifles of the dead. Although they had plenty of K-rations, so they didn't go hungry, the defenders had had no sleep for over twenty-four hours. Something had to be done at Dornot, and soon.

★ ★ ★

Colonel Paddy had had enough. The brutality of the Germans and the treachery of their so-called allies of the *Maquis* repelled him. The latter he regarded as little better than cut-throats. A contemporary report by one of Mayne's officers, Lieutenant Riding, put it in a nutshell: 'Their main desire seemed to be to get arms and hold the local farmers (or anyone else against whom they held a grudge) to ransom. They had no discipline or organization and went to pieces when attacked.'

Since 29 August, when he had landed in France, Mayne had led four parties of reinforcements for his Regiment which was holed up in the Forest of Fontainebleau through German lines, risking being ambushed all the time. On one occasion he and a group of 'new boys' were rolling down a country lane when they heard the sound of motors. Before the little convoy could back up or go off the road a six-wheeled German armoured car came round the bend in front of them, its long cannon pointing in their direction.

'Pull up,' Mayne yelled.

Even before the driver could brake, Mayne was pelting down the side of the hedge, two grenades in his hands. He ducked just where he had guessed the armoured car would stop and fire its cannon, but the German gunner never had a chance. The next moment the grenades exploded underneath the vehicle. It rose into the air and slammed down again in a flurry of dust and the engine went up in flames. No one got out. Mayne jumped into the jeep without another word, as if he destroyed German armoured cars every day of the week.

But in addition to his disgust at the conduct of the Germans and the *Maquis*, Mayne could see that his survivors were getting very tired and some of the more recent recruits were beginning to crack under the stress. It was understandable. They had been operating in the heart of enemy territory for weeks. Even the most stupid of his troopers knew that they would be tortured and murdered if they were captured and death at the hands of an enemy bullet stalked them daily. He also knew that surly *Maquisards* who had been disciplined by him and his officers were just waiting for a chance to plunge a knife into his back. It was time to withdraw.

So the survivors set off in captured German armoured troop-carriers, cheered by the citizens of the little towns they passed through, for they had been sorely plagued by the thieving *Maquisards* and Paddy Mayne's imposing presence had frightened the Maquis into some semblance of order.

The SAS's losses had been high, but they had done the job that Eisenhower's planners had set for them and the Supreme Commander was the first to acknowledge this. In a letter he wrote to Brigadier McLeod, the commander of the 1st SAS Brigade, he sent his 'congratulations to all ranks of the Special Air Service Brigade on the contribution which they have made to the success of the Allied Expeditionary Force.

'The ruthlessness with which the enemy have attacked Special Air Service troops has been an indication of the injury you were able to cause the German armed forces both by your own efforts and by the information which you gave of German dispositions and movements.

'Many Special Air Service troops are still behind enemy lines; others are being reformed for new tasks. To all of them I say "Well done and good luck!"'

Eisenhower was right. There were still Brian Franks and what was left of his 2nd SAS Regiment being driven, fighting all the way, into the Vosges Mountains and the advancing US 7th Army. But before they finally got away a terrible price would have to be paid for their escape.

As the 5th Infantry Division had by now established another bridgehead across the Meuse at Arnaville, though Patton's other divisions, the 79th, 80th, 35th and 4th Armored had not been able to follow suit, it was decided to abandon the costly Dornot bridgehead. Because of radio silence, two swimmers carried the withdrawal order across to Captain Gerrie on the other side.

The plan was to withdraw that night at a quarter past nine. Ropes, supported by floats, were now stretched across the river as soon as it was dark and a few leaky boats and dinghies were assembled by the engineers. Further infantry were stealthily brought up to the west bank to give the withdrawing men covering fire. When everyone had cleared the eastern bank a Lieutenant Marshall and his signals sergeant would fire green flares. These would be the signal for the divisional artillery to plaster the area of Horseshoe Wood in the hope that by then it would be full of advancing Germans.

The evacuation began in pitch darkness. Over the German positions flares sailed into the night. It was clear that the Germans suspected something was going on. But Captain Gerrie had no time to concern himself with that worrying thought. He was too busy supervising the loading of the badly wounded into the handful of boats. Others had already waded into the icy water to begin crossing by the rope or, if they could, swim the Meuse.

More and more GIs slipped into the water: 'E' Company sixty men and no surviving officers; 'K' Company fifty men and no officers. On the eastern bank three officers, including Marshall, crept through the darkness checking that no one had been left behind. Suddenly they froze. There was the rusty rattle of tank tracks and there were no American tanks across the Meuse.

'Krauts', Marshall hissed.

The three officers started to back off towards the river. Suddenly one of the German tanks fired a green flare, a signal to the German infantry following them. The whole weight of the divisional artillery thundered into action, thinking that this was the signal that the evacuation was completed. The three officers began to run as German shells fell on the river and their own guns began to 'walk' across from Dornot towards Horseshoe Ridge.

Soaked and exhausted, the survivors were hurried through a burning

Dornot up the steep cobbled road to where cognac, hot coffee and food awaited them.

The butcher's bill was high. A total of 945 men were killed, missing or wounded. Many more succumbed to exhaustion and combat fatigue afterwards. The 5th Division's 11th Infantry had effectively lost a whole battalion. The Seventh Armored's 23rd Armored Infantry Battalion, which had been in action for four days, also suffered over 200 casualties and had to be withdrawn for refitting and reinforcing.

Just before dawn on 11 September, 1944, Private Joseph Lewakowski awoke from a deep sleep in his foxhole on the eastern bank of the River Meuse to find the battlefield abandoned. There was hardly a sound save for the rumble of heavy guns at the other bridgehead of Arnaville. He had slept through everything. Now his comrades had gone. He shook his head and rubbed his unshaven chin. What was he going to do? He decided he'd try to make it back by himself. He clambered out of his foxhole, which was protected by a roof of logs and dirt, and began to walk across dead Germans who lay in a solid grey carpet from his hole to the river. There he found the rope. Stepping into the water, he started to pull himself across. That young private was the last one back at Dornot. Patton had received his first bloody nose of the campaign. It would not be the last in the mud and blood of the Lorraine Campaign. But there was worse to come on this wet and cold Monday. *Somebody else would beat him to the Siegfried Line!*

4

INTO THE REICH

On that afternoon of Monday, 11 September the local burgomaster of the little village of Sevenig on the River Our, the border village between Luxemburg and Germany, was sitting on a bench outside his house, smoking what the Germans call *eine Shagpfeife*. It had grown warm again and there was some sun. Although the war had been raging for nearly five years now and he had heard that the *Wehrmacht* was retreating towards Germany, Burgomaster Michel Weber thought how peaceful everything looked. The ripe corn was yellow in heaps formed around poles, the birds were singing and the little border river, which anyone could wade through at this time, bubbled below. Weber gave a contented puff at his pipe, at peace with the world. Things weren't so bad for Germany after all.

Suddenly he was alerted by the sound of men splashing through the shallows from Luxemburg heading for the German side. He sat up. A German captain in a tattered uniform was heading towards him, followed by two privates, as ragged and as dusty as he was.

The *Hauptmann*, his face red and angry, clambered up the bank and stared down at the old Burgomaster. '*Was*,' he rasped, '*Sie sind noch hier?*'*

Michel Weber took the pipe out of his mouth. What did the captain mean? The officer enlightened him in a moment. 'Save yourself. We're the last ones. After us the enemy's coming!'

Before Weber could ask any questions, the captain and two soldiers were panting up the slope beyond to vanish into the trees, leaving Weber to ponder what he had meant. Did the captain mean that they were the last of some decimated infantry battalion? Or had he meant they were

* What, you're still here?

last of the broken army which had defended France? Were things really that bad?

The Burgomaster stared up at the wooded heights on the Luxemburg side of the river. There was no sound save that of the September wind in the trees and the ripple of the stream below. Then he saw them filtering through the trees. He knew immediately that something was wrong. If they had been a German patrol he would hear the grating of their steel-shod jackboots. These men were making no sound whatsoever. They were wearing rubber-soled shoes. These were Americans.

Moving swiftly for one accustomed to taking everything in his stride, he hurried into the hamlet to find the *Dorfschreier*, the local man who rang his bell to alert the villagers to important announcements. Hurriedly he gasped, '*Die Amis sind da!*'*

* * *

Some five hours after Weber had spotted the first *Amis* on the Luxemburg side of the River Our, Sergeant Warner H. Holzinger was told by his C.O. Lieutenant Vipond of the US 5th Armored Division's 85th Reconnaissance Squadron's Troop 'B' that if he wished to claim the credit for being the first enemy soldier to enter Germany since Napoleon nearly 150 years before he'd better hurry. All three divisions of General Gerow's V Corps, now supporting Patton – the 4th Infantry, their own 5th Armored and the 28th Infantry – were vying with each other to get to the Siegfried Line first. The men who did it would make headlines throughout the free world.

Holzinger of 'B' Squadron's Second Troop decided to have a go. Accompanied by Corporal Ralph Diven, Sergeant Locke, Pfcs William McCollingan, George McNeal, Jesse Stevens and their French interpreter, Lionel Delille, he went down the steep country road from the Luxemburg heights to the hamlet of Stolzemburg, where the locals told him there were no German soldiers in the area any more. They were also told that they would see the first bunkers of the Siegfried Line if they went up to the heights on the German side.

They crossed the Our at a weir and came to the hamlet of Gmuend. The hamlet seemed deserted. It was as if the war had already ended. They came across the first bunker (it's still there) dug into the base of the rocky height covering the river. It was empty. So this was the vaunted Siegfried

* The Americans are here.

31

Line — a bush-and-weed-covered slab of concrete with an iron-framed slit for some small-calibre weapon!

The little group pushed on. They came across another bunker higher up, also empty. They climbed the steep curving road to the heights. In front of them stretched a rolling high plateau, empty of troops, though dominated by other, larger bunkers. For a while they explored as the shadows lengthened, finding some twenty-odd pillboxes, all empty, their guns long gone, the grey dust thick on the floors, as if they hadn't been occupied since May, 1940, when Hitler had marched westwards. It seemed as if the Siegfried Line, the Reich's last bastion, was yet another of Dr Goebbels' propaganda tricks.

Now it was beginning to get dark. Holzinger had no desire to stay any longer in Germany. The first Allied soldier to penetrate Hitler's Reich gave the order to beat it back to the other side of the River Our.

Thirty minutes later an excited Sergeant Holzinger was relating his discoveries to Lieutenant Vipond. Sixty minutes after that the information was on its way to no less a person than General Courtney Hodges, to whose army the Fifth Armored Division belonged. That Monday night Hodges' First Army issued a statement in the unemotional prose of the military. It read: 'At 1805 hrs on 11 September, a patrol led by S.Sgt Warner H. Holzinger crossed into Germany near the village of Stolzemburg, a few miles north-east of Vianden, Luxemburg.'

*   *   *

Patton fumed. His 'sure thing', as he had called his attack on Germany, had not paid off. He was stalled on the River Moselle with his lead troops still twenty-five miles from the Siegfried Line. Hodges, the plodding infantryman whom he considered 'dumb' and 'also very jealous of me', had beaten him to be the first to enter Germany. It was all very frustrating.

But that night patrols of the 28th Infantry Division, which also belonged to First Army's V Corps, crossed from the Luxemburg village of Weiswampach down to the German village of Sevenig, where Burgomaster Weber was still wondering what he should do. They brought back with them some worthless German marks, a peaked black farmer's cap and some bottles of German earth to show that they had actually been there.

That night a strong reconnaissance patrol from the 4th Infantry Division's 22nd Regiment under the command of 1st Lieutenant Robert Manning was selected to do the same. The patrol consisted of five jeeps and one self-propelled gun. Their mission was to obtain information about the enemy and collect a jar full of German earth which would be forwarded to President Roosevelt. The Fourth always had a keen eye for publicity.

After a journey of eight miles the little patrol started to descend the steep track towards the River Our. They discovered that the railway bridge which linked Belgium and Germany at the hamlet of Hemmeres had been blown. As the self-propelled gun could not cross the river, the two officers with the patrol, Manning and Shugart, tossed a coin to see who would lead a foot patrol across the Our into Hemmeres. Shugart won and crossed into Germany that night at half past nine.

Although both the 5th Armored and the 28th Infantry had beaten the Fourth across, Captain Stevenson, the Division's publicity officer, was quicker off the mark with his press release. Under the headline 'Crackers of the Hindenburg Line, First to break Siegfried Line,' the US Army paper *Stars and Stripes* reported, 'The US 4th Infantry Division, the first American Army outfit to crack the Hindenburg Line at Meuse-Argonne in the last war and first to enter Paris in this one, also was the first to penetrate Germany through the Siegfried Line in force, it was revealed today.'

Now things were moving fast for the Fourth, nicknamed the 'Ivy League Division' on account of its divisional patch. Further strong patrols from the 22nd Infantry crossed the Our. On the morning of Tuesday, 12 September, the 44th Field Artillery Battalion fired the first light shells into Germany. Again Captain Stevenson proudly proclaimed these were the 'first shells to strike Germany proper'. They weren't. The US 1st Division, 'the Big Red One', had already done that further north in the Aachen region.

Then at quarter to nine that morning Colonel Lanham, the commander of the 22nd Regiment, ordered the whole regiment to move into Germany and seize the high ground beyond the Our. With them the regimental column would take a bearded, bespectacled war correspondent, who was the best publicist of all for the Fourth Infantry Regiment. His name was Ernest Hemingway.

*　　*　　*

That morning as Hemingway and the regimental column headed towards the Reich a second patrol from the 5th Armored Division, under the command of Lieutenant Vipond, crossed the Our and climbed the steep hill to the bunkers which Holzinger had inspected the evening before. But this time they came back in a hurry. As Vipond told his superior officer, 'We spotted about sixty Krauts. They carried bundles and machine guns. At every bunker they stopped and dropped off six to ten men.' The Germans seemed to be at ease and did not notice the American scouts. Vipond's report was rushed to divisional headquarters. It was vital, for it made clear that the Germans were occupying the Siegfried Line once more after four years of absence.

Hemingway, with the 22nd Infantry, knew nothing of it. To him it seemed that the Germans, what there were of them, were in full retreat out of the Siegfried Line positions. As he recorded for *Collier's Magazine*: 'I saw two enemy half-tracks tearing up the white road that led into the German hills. . . . American artillery shells began dropping around them. You watched one half-track slither sideways across the road. The other stopped on the turn of the road after trying twice to move like a wounded animal. Another shell pounded up a fountain of dust and smoke alongside the crippled half-track and when the smoke cleared you could see the bodies on the road. That was the end of the rat race.' To Hemingway it seemed all too easy.

So they came to Hemmeres in Germany, a small untidy riverside hamlet of dirty white houses grouped around a small chapel, and a few tumbledown farms, with manure heaps under the kitchen windows. Ugly women and ill-shaped men 'came sidling up to the Americans, holding their hands up in surrender or bearing bottles of schnapps some of which they drank themselves to prove that the liquor wasn't poisoned.'

While Lanham's men swarmed forward to the next ridge line, which the Division would be still fighting for six months later, Hemingway found a farmhouse at the edge of the hamlet which he took over.

That evening Lanham arrived with his three battalion commanders and discussed the plan for the morrow while Hemingway and a Brazilian war correspondent nicknamed 'Bazilius' poured the drinks. That night the correspondents and the soldiers dined in style. There was 'chicken, peas, fresh onions, carrots, salad and canned fruit'.

As Colonel Lanham recalled afterwards, it was 'my happiest night of the whole war. The food was excellent, the wine plentiful, the comradeship close and warm. It was a night to put aside the thought of the great West Wall against which we would throw ourselves within the next forty-eight hours. We laughed and drank and told horrendous stories about each other. We all seemed for a moment like minor gods and

Hemingway, presiding at the head of the table, might have been a fatherly Mars delighting in the happiness of his brood.'

The attack on the Siegfried Line was about to begin. This was to be the last happy day.

★   ★   ★

Twelve days previously draconian measures had been applied throughout the Third Reich to prepare the country for the battle of the frontier soon to come. That day all theatres, music halls, cabarets and schools of music were shut. All publishers were closed down, save those publishing school books and the one which brought out the Fuhrer's *Mein Kampf*. All university departments, save those of medicine, were also closed. The *Luftwaffe* was ordered to stop training pilots. The pilots and their ground crews would be needed for the infantry.

It was the same with the German Navy. All capital ships were ordered to be mothballed. Their crews and those of the Submarine arm, which no longer had submarines, were also sent to the infantry.

Everywhere throughout the Reich, military hospitals and depots were combed for 'bodies'. 'Stomach Battalions', made up of men who had been wounded in the stomach or had severe stomach complaints, were set up and grouped in 'Whitebread Divisions', so named because the men were given white bread for the sake of their stomachs instead of the usual black hard bread of the Army, *das Kommisbrot*.

'Ear and Nose Battalions' followed. They were made up of men who had one or both ears missing or were very deaf. In such battalions orders often had to be given by sign language. Service in these battalions was particularly dangerous. The men couldn't hear incoming fire and at night sentries often shot their own guard commanders when they appeared suddenly and, for them, noiselessly.

When these desperate measures were announced publicly by Berlin, the Press of the Free World had a field day, mocking 'Germany's *Volksturm* made up of old men, stomach cases, cripples with glass eyes and wooden legs'.

The GIs who would soon attack the Siegfried Line didn't think it funny at all. As one of them told the Army magazine *Yank*, 'I don't care if the guy behind the gun is a syphilitic prick who is a hundred years old, he's still sitting behind eight feet of concrete and he's still got enough fingers to press triggers and shoot bullets.'

Soon hundreds of thousands of young men, green but fit for the most part, would be formed in *Volksgrenadier* Battalions and in due course the

People's Grenadier Battalions would become divisions. They might not have been the best infantrymen in the world, but they were plentifully supplied with the latest automatic weapons and large numbers of self-propelled guns. Mostly importantly, they were led by officers who had been learning their profession on the battlefield for years when most American infantry officers, regular or otherwise, were stuck in some remote garrison, where the highpoint of the week was getting drunk in the officers' club on a Saturday night.

Directing these new formations would be generals who had fought tremendous battles in Russia, the like of which American generals could not even conceive. One such was 69-year-old Field Marshal von Rundstedt, who was being summoned now to take charge of the Siegfried Line defences. He told his interrogators after the war, 'I knew there was no chance of winning the war, but I hoped that if I held on long enough a shift in political events might save Germany from complete collapse.'

No matter that he had swallowed Goebbels' fiction that sooner or later the Anglo-American-Russian alliance would break down, he *did* believe that he might be able to save Germany in her eleventh hour. He knew he had to buy time. If he could stop the Americans at the Siegfried Line then he would have achieved that objective. In the first week of September 200,000 boys and girls of the Hitler Youth, along with old men and Russian prisoners, were shipped to the Line to prepare it for what was to come. Time was running out fast. But Patton had been stopped on the Moselle, forty kilometres away from the Line. If Rundstedt could stop these first *Amis* crossing the River Our there still might be hope for his beloved Germany.

Just behind the Siegfried Line, however, on that 11 September when Sergeant Holzinger led the first patrol across the Our, something akin to panic reigned. While the Nazi commanders tried frantically to evacuate the local peasants, equally frantically the *Wehrmacht* attempted to send 'March Battalions' and 'Alarm Battalions' to man the Line.

In Trier alone, the biggest town to the rear of the Line, there were some 40,000 German soldiers, stragglers, deserters and others cut off from their units as they had fled through France, Belgium and Luxemburg. They were without leadership and so far only one battalion – 'Battalion Trier', commanded by another former priest, this time a Catholic one – was currently on its way to the front.

'Today,' one young soldier wrote in his diary, 'I was transferred to the 42nd Machine Gun Fortress Battalion as a messenger, destination West

Wall. This battalion is composed of Home Guard, soldiers and half-cripples. I found many among them who were obviously off mentally. Some had their arms amputated, others had one leg short. A sad sight.'

All the same, as General Keppler's 1st SS Corps took up its positions around the Eifel township of Prum, just behind the Siegfried Line in that part of it which Gerow's US V Corps would attack, Field Marshal von Rundstedt was relatively sanguine.

At his headquarters some seventy miles away at the confluence of the Rhine and the Moselle on the heights above Coblenz, von Rundstedt now learned that his troops were already beginning to man the Siegfried Line bunkers and that the Americans had not yet attacked. Wise in the ways of war, the wrinkled old soldier reasoned that, although he might be deficient in troops and weapons, his men did have the protection afforded them by the thick ferro-concrete of their bunkers. In defence it would take three attackers for every defender; that was the standard formula. Besides, he knew from his Intelligence that the *Amis* had little experience in attacking fortified positions. That was not their style.

Von Rundstedt would have been even more confident if he had known exactly who would be manning the Line in the area where Gerow's 4th and 28th Infantry Divisions would start their assault. For here, somewhat depleted and with few armoured vehicles left, was assembled the 2nd SS Panzer Division, *Das Reich*, which Mayne's 1st SAS Regiment had delayed reaching the Normandy front back in July. *Das Reich* was one of the most elite formations in the whole German Army. If anyone was going to stop the Americans in their first attempt to break through the Siegfried Line it would be *Das Reich*.

On the same day that what was left of the *Das Reich* went into the line von Rundstedt issued an order of the day. It read: 'The West Wall will play a decisive role in the battle for Germany. The West Wall bunkers will be defended to the last bullet and man, even if it means self-destruction.' Von Rundstedt added that this order had come from the Führer himself. But it was an order that was wasted on the men of *Das Reich*. They were prepared to fight to the last bullet and the last man as it was — *and they would!*

5

PAPA GOES TO WAR

On the evening of Wednesday 13 September Colonel 'Buck' Lanham, commander of the Fourth Division's 22nd Regiment, assembled his officers in the tiny hamlet of Schweiler, just across the border into Germany. In the hissing light of Coleman lanterns – there was no electricity or running water for that matter – he briefed his officers, while Hemingway looked on. The novelist had quartered himself in a little farm in the same village, lived in by peasants with a pretty daughter, whom they made sleep between them at night to prevent her being raped. Not that Hemingway was in a position to do that. At the age of forty-five he was already impotent!

Lanham's scouts had discovered that the enemy held the ridge called '*der Schwarzer Mann*' (the Black Man), which was heavily fortified with bunkers, leading to the village of Brandscheid which had been integrated into the Siegfried Line, with no less than eight bunkers concealed around the village. By the time Brandscheid was finally captured in February, 1945, it would be known as the 'German Verdun'.

Lanham's plan was to attack at ten o'clock on the following morning. The Regiment would attack in a column of battalions. The 3rd Battalion would lead and assemble at the village of Buchet to the north of Brandscheid. From there it was to work its way through the first line of fortifications. It would be followed by Lanham's 1st Battalion which would advance through the gap blown in the Siegfried Line by its sister regiment. Lanham would keep his 2nd Battalion in reserve just in case the Germans counter-attacked, though, as the briefing ended just before midnight, he though that there was little possibility of that.

It all seemed cut and dried. But the bespectacled Colonel would not have been so sanguine if he had known that 'Battle Group Kuehne', named after its commander, Major Kuehne, was waiting for him. Two days before Kuehne had organized his Group from a collection of boys and convalescents at the barracks at Wittlich to the rear. From Prum the Battle Group had been rushed to the West Wall in the half-tracks of *Das Reich*. Now Kuehne's boys and sick men, stiffened by some SS troopers, prepared to take on the first attack on the Siegfried Line by the US Army.

At first all went well that Thursday morning. Covered by their own artillery fire, the men of Lanham's 3rd Battalion, well spread out, advanced across the open fields and through the woods leading to the heights. The German line was silent. Perhaps, the men hoped, the enemy had already abandoned it.

Suddenly the Germans of Battle Group Kuehne and the SS reacted. There was that familiar hiss of Spandaus, firing 1,000 rounds a minute. Mortars cracked and howled, followed by the frightening sound of an 80mm shell. The attack started to bog down.

As Hemingway described it, 'They started coming back down across the field, dragging a few wounded, and a few limping. You know how they look coming back. Then the tanks started coming back and the TD's coming back and the men coming back plenty. They couldn't stay in that bare field and the ones who weren't hit started yelling for the medics for those who were hit and you know that excites everybody.'

Captain Howard Blazzard of the 3rd Battalion, watching the battle with Colonel Lanham, snapped, 'Sir, I can go out there and kick those bastards in the tail and take that place.'

Lanham shouted back, 'You're an S-2 [operations officer] in a staff function and you stay where you are.'

Blazzard fell silent, but as more and more men began to drift back he told himself, 'We're going to lose this battle.'

Lanham must have felt the same for suddenly he cried, 'Let's get up there! This thing has got to move. Those chickenspitters aren't going to break down this attack.'

Lanham, with his pistol drawn, followed by Blazzard, moved forward to where his men were taking cover in a fold in the ground. 'Let's get up there,' he cried, 'and get this place taken.'

He fired a couple of shots in the general direction of the Germans to encourage his reluctant heroes. 'Goddam, let's get these Krauts. Come on. Nobody's going to stop here now!'

He kept on shouting, threatening, until finally his men got up and advanced into the woods at the top of the slope. Then darkness fell and, in order to avoid confusion and men firing on their comrades, Lanham ordered his soldiers to dig in for the night. On the morrow they would change the direction of the attack and assault Brandscheid.

While his men rested and ate cold K-rations, Lanham pondered the problem of assaulting the bunkers and pillboxes of the Line. Back in England before D-Day the 4th Division had been taught how to assault bunkers. But those men were long gone, dead, wounded or missing (in the first month after D-Day, the 22nd Regiment had suffered 3439 casualties). The men under his command now were used to a war of pursuit, not of assault. In the end Lanham decided he would have to use his handful of attached tank destroyers to blast their way through the bunker line.

It was something which delighted Hemingway. It appealed to his sense of *grand guignol* and juvenile blood lust. The 'wump guns', as he called the tank destroyers, were just the thing for him. 'The Krauts wouldn't come out,' he wrote for his magazine, 'when talked to, so we pulled that TD right up to the back of that steel door we had located by now and that old Wump gun fired about six rounds and blasted the door in and you ought to have heard them wanting to come out. You ought to have heard them yell and moan and moan and scream and yell *Kamerad*. . . . They started to come out and you never saw such a mess. Every one of them was wounded in five or six places from pieces of concrete and steel. About eighteen men came out and they got down on their knees on the road. They expected to get shot. But we were obliged to disappoint them. . . . There were legs and arms scattered all over the goddamn place.'

But though the men of Battle Group Kuehne were suffering heavy casualties (only 120 survived of the original 800), Lanham's men were taking heavy casualties too, as were the men of his sister regiments, the 8th and the 12th Infantry. As soon as the attack was resumed on the following morning the 22nd Regiment was hit by a spirited counter-attack. Colonel Dowdy, commanding Lanham's 1st Battalion, was killed. His Company 'A' was beaten back in some disorder. In the end they withdrew to their starting point with only two officers and sixty-six men left. That meant that they had suffered fifty per cent casualties. Slowly the steam was beginning to go out of the 22nd Regiment's attack.

Already the first cases of combat fatigue, which would soon become endemic on that distant frontier, had begun to occur, and not only among the rank and file. As the US Department of Defense's official war history notes for 17 September when the 1st Battalion resumed its attack under a new Commander, Major Latimer: 'Enemy shelling so unnerved several officers, including the Commander of the attacked tank platoon, that they had to be evacuated for combat exhaustion. About 0830, as Company 'A' moved to the line of departure, another severe shelling so upset the Company Commander that he, too, had to be evacuated.'

By Sunday Lanham's attack was effectively stalled. He ordered his battered 1st Battalion to withdraw. At HQ the Fourth's Assistant Divisional Commander, Brigadier-General George Taylor, drove to Corps headquarters at Eupen in Belgium to report on the situation. There he told General Gerow, who would soon be returning to the States, that the 4th had suffered heavy casualties for the six-mile gap it had managed to make in the Siegfried Line. But no significant ground had been captured to justify the casualties it had suffered. Wasn't it time to halt the division and let it 're-group' for a while? Gerow agreed. The Fourth Division would now go over to 'aggressive defence'.

Hemingway always knew when a good story had died. He left to return to his 'command post' at the Hotel Ritz in Paris.

★   ★   ★

On the Fourth Division's right flank the 'Bloody Bucket' (as the 28th Infantry Division was known from its divisional patch, which looked like a bucket full of blood, and its reputation for suffering horrific casualties) was attacking from Luxemburg into Germany. Here the Division faced the best the Germans had – the *Panzergrenadier Regiment der Führer* – the 2nd SS Panzer Division. It was to be expected that the SS troopers would resist to the last, and they did.

The two regiments attacking, the 109th and 110th, were involved in heavy fighting right from the start. On the first day of their attack over Ihren Creek towards the pillboxes of the Siegfried Line to their front, they were stopped dead 700 yards away. Towed tank destroyers were whistled up. But their indirect fire did little to the pillboxes but 'dust off the camouflage', as one observer reported.

The next day the advance continued, but the two regiments kept losing men to mines and enemy fire from the thick-walled bunkers. The fields leading towards the heights were littered with dead infantrymen.

They came to the first of the dragon's teeth which protected the bunkers from armoured attack. Lieutenant Joseph Dew brought his Sherman to within a few feet of the concrete obstacles and blasted a path through them with his 75mm gun.

Again the advance continued. But progress was painfully slow and the two regiments were taking hundreds of casualties daily. On 16

September, just after the men of Colonel Seely's 110th Infantry had captured a series of pillboxes and, exhausted as they were, were settling down for the night, Private Roy Fleming was alerted by a strange lull in the usual nightly barrage. 'Suddenly everything became quiet. I could hear the clank of these vehicles. I saw a flame-thrower start and heard the sounds of a helluva scrap up around Captain Schultz's positions.'

A few minutes after the sentry heard the first sounds of the surprise German counter-attack another company intercepted a frantic radio message in clear instead of in code. 'KING SUGAR to anybody. KING SUGAR to anybody. Help. We are having a counter-attack.' But before the Regiment could react the noise had subsided and the radio had gone dead.

Nothing was ever discovered about what had happened to the Regiment's 'F' Company, though there was a rumour that the Germans had attacked with improvised flame-throwers mounted on the 2nd SS's half-tracks. But the fact that virtually a whole company had disappeared took the heart out of the 28th's attack.

But on 16 September the commander of the Division's 110th Regiment threw in his 1st Battalion which had been in reserve up to now. Supported by tanks, the 1st made good progress. It recaptured the pillboxes lost by the missing 'F' Company and pushed forward on a narrow front to capture the most commanding ground of the area. As the official US military history of the Siegfried Line campaign states truly, 'Though the penetration was narrow and pencil-like, the 28th Division had for all practical purposes broken through the West Wall.'

But the 28th Division had lived up to its nickname of 'Bloody Bucket'. By now it had suffered 1,500 casualties, all infantrymen, and infantrymen were in short supply. So it was that on the same day the Division broke through the Siegfried Line, the Corps Commander, General Gerow, arrived at the 28th's HQ to order the attack to be stopped. The 109th and 110th were in no shape to exploit the breakthrough and there were no other troops available in Gerow's V Corps to help out. In effect the first American attack on the Siegfried Line was slowly coming to an end.

*   *   *

Surprisingly enough, it was the secondary attack of Gerow's 5th Armored Division, with the 28th Division's 112th Infantry Regiment, which in the end proved the most promising. On 14 September the 'Victory Division', as it proudly called itself, crossed the River Sauer (Sûre in French) in the area of the Luxemburg town of Wallendorf.

German resistance was weak. Rapidly the tanks and infantry pressed forward to the towering heights above the river where primitive man had once dwelled in the many caves which can still be seen up there.

Next morning the 5th Armored's leading elements bumped into a German company of Mark IV tanks supported by infantry. The Sherman gunners went into action straightaway while the Germans were still recovering from their surprise at meeting the enemy so far into Germany. The first German tank was hit before the enemy could get off a shot. This was a battle that the Americans would win for a change. One after another the Sherman gunners knocked out three enemy tanks and six halftracks, packed with infantry. It was too much for the rest of the German force. The five remaining Mark IVs scurried away to the safety of the woods. The Americans pushed on into what came to be known as 'Deadman's Creek'. By nightfall the Fifth Armored had left the Siegfried Line behind and were six miles deep into German territory.

The news that the *Amis* had penetrated so deep into Germany even alarmed von Rundstedt. By sheer chance the Americans had struck at a spot where the axis lay between Field Marshal Model's northern Army Group B and General von Blaskowitz's Army Group G. This meant that operations against the Americans in the Wallendorf area would be conducted by two headquarters which were over 150 miles away from each other. Von Rundstedt took personal command of the defence for a while so that the administrative problems could be sorted out. In the meantime he threw in anything and everything he could find to stop the Americans advancing on their next objective, Bitburg, from which they obviously intended to race for the Rhine.*

Another *Alarm Battalion Trier*, again commanded by a former pastor, Captain Karl Kornowski, was rushed to the front. At the first village they came to Kornowski was advised by a fellow priest to 'take off your grey uniform and put on your priest's robe.' Kornowski answered, 'It's too early for that.' So he went on with his men. In the confused state of the German front he came across a major from a panzer division who ordered him to attack. 'Where?' Kornowski asked the major who was cowering fearfully in a foxhole. 'Up front,' came the answer. 'But where's the front?' he asked. He got no answer, for, as Kornowski related later in not exactly the language one could expect from a priest, 'the tit was too busy crapping his pants to show us'.

---

* In the event it would be from Bitburg that Patton's Fourth Armored Division did race for the Rhine, reaching it in just over fifty hours: but that would be *six* months later.

The Alarm Battalion went on towards Deadman's Creek, in fact the valley of the River Gay. There they were to recapture nine bunkers taken by the enemy. But the American defenders proved too powerful for the Alarm Battalion. Kornowski was ordered to withdraw, which he and his men did with difficulty. There seemed to be *Amis* everywhere. But the ex-priest didn't make it. He ran into an American ambush. When he saw the '*Ami* pointing his rifle at me, I raised my hands in surrender. Two Americans escorted me back towards Wallendorf.' There he was met by another group of US infantry. They stopped him and looted him of his possessions, which included a bottle of schnapps given to him by the priest who had suggested he should desert. 'First I had to take a drink to show it wasn't poisoned, then it went the round of the victors' throats. But they did give me back my tobacco pouch, rosary and picture of the Virgin Mary. Nice of them.'

One wonders if the ex-priest's comment was meant to be sarcastic. At all events he survived to become a local Eifel priest for another forty years.

But on the day the former captain of infantry from Trier was captured General Gerow gave the order to stop the attack from Wallendorf. As usual this decision was supposed to be based on the lack of supplies, which (in American eyes at least) were all going to Montgomery, who would soon launch his abortive Operation 'Market Garden', to 'bounce' his way into Germany, which ended in the disaster of Arnhem.

But was it as simple as that?

We know that part of the fault was Eisenhower's 'Broad Front Strategy'. We also know that neither Hodges nor Patton abided by the decisions taken at Chartres on 2 September. Both encouraged their corps commanders to keep on going in the hope that they might make it through the Siegfried Line and be the first Allied troops to enter Germany.

But were supplies diverted from Patton and Hodges in order that Montgomery should succeed in the north? It has always been the contention of American historians of the Second World War that they were.

Both Hodges' First and Patton's Third Army were supplied by the 'Red Ball' Express, trucks manned by black drivers who sped up to the front taking on average five tons of supplies per truck. But who supplied the British, especially with petrol and diesel which came through the British 'Pluto' pipeline from the UK to the beaches where the trucks picked up the vital fuel that was needed for a mechanized army? More especially, who delivered it to the British before and during the Market Garden operation, which the American generals always blamed for the lack of gasoline?

The answer is *not* the Red Ball Express. Instead, four days after both Hodges and Patton had reported to General Bradley on 12 September that *both their armies had sufficient gasoline and ammunition to carry them to the Rhine*, the Red Lion convoys, which would supply the Anglo-American airborne army, started to roll from Normandy to Brussels. But the Red Lion was organized and staffed by the British 2nd Army. It did, however, involve eight US transportation companies.

The Red Lion Express performed a little better than the Red Ball. It carried more fuel than the Americans (650 tons in contrast to 500 tons in the case of the average US convoy) and was quicker and more efficient due to the fact all its supplies were picked up from one dump only and deposited again at a single dump. As the official US Department of Defense history states: 'Red Lion convoys exceeded their target . . . and handled a total of 18,000 tons. Almost half of this consisted of supplies for the two US airborne divisions participating in the Holland operation, a statistic often ignored by the partisans who so heatedly criticized this 'diversion' of US resources. Furthermore the operation took place *after* the pursuit had definitely been halted and both the First and Third US Armies had come up against the prepared defenses of the West Wall.'

What had stopped the 1st and 3rd US Armies? Not the machinations of Montgomery. Simply the stubborn German defence.

★   ★   ★

On that Saturday, 16 September, 1944, when Gerow decided to halt his V Corps, Adolf Hitler asked his most trusted generals to the 'Wolf' in East Prussia.

First to enter was Field Marshal Keitel, despised by the other generals because he was Hitler's toady. He was followed by General Jodl, Hitler's Chief of Operations. Finally in came Hitler. His eyes were watery and his mouth loose and slack.

Although Keitel was in command, it was Jodl, as usual, who did the briefing. He presented the ugly facts of the war in his normal precise manner, hiding nothing. Germany was friendless. Italy was finished. Japan had politely suggested through the Japanese Ambassador, Baron Oshima, that the Third Reich should start armistice negotiations with Russia. Germany's Rumanian and Bulgarian allies had just changed sides and joined the Russians. The Finns, perhaps Germany's best and most loyal allies, had just broken with the Reich.

Then Jodl addressed himself to the fronts in Italy, the East and West. As he came to the Western Front, he showed a glimmer of optimism. The British, he said, were still busy clearing up the Channel coast, four hundred kilometres from Germany's frontiers, Patton was stalled on the Meuse, adding, 'And on the Western Front we are getting a real rest in the Ardennes.'

At the mention of the Ardennes Hitler suddenly came to life. He sat up and, raising his arm dramatically, he cried, 'Stop'.

The generals stared. For two long minutes Hitler said nothing. Then he broke the silence. 'I have made a momentous decision. I am taking the offensive. Here – out of the Ardennes.' He smashed his fist on the unrolled map before him. 'Across the Meuse and on to Antwerp!'

The generals stared at him in silent awe. This was the old Hitler, the Führer of that great year of victories, 1940. Suddenly a wave of new confidence swept through the inner chamber. Perhaps Germany had a chance after all.

6

COUNTER-ATTACK

First she stepped into the special undergarment of heavy silk. Then her assistant fastened its thin inner belt around her slim waist. After this she secured the triangular piece of elastic attached to the undergarment between her slender legs, rumoured to be insured for a million dollars, adjusting it to fit between the sides of her shaven vulva to minimize the pain of the tension to come. Bending over so that her drooping breasts hung clear of her body, she scooped them in turn into the garment's specially re-inforced cups. Holding them firmly, checking that the nipples were in the correct place, she waited while her assistant zipped her up. Moments later a sequinned sheath was pulled over her blonde head and she was almost ready. Marlene Dietrich was in business. In a minute she could go out and entertain the waiting troops of Patton's Third Army.

She had arrived at General Patton's headquarters on 16 September, shortly after Dinah Shaw and Bing Crosby, who had also come to entertain Patton's men in a short lull in the fighting. Patton had looked down at her and asked, 'If you really had the courage to face the danger of going to the front, could you take it?'

Marlene said she could, but she was afraid of what the Nazis would do to her if they captured her. Patton smiled and said, 'They wouldn't waste you. If you're captured, it's more likely that you would be utilized for propaganda, forced to make radio broadcasts like you did for us.' Then he took a small gun from the pocket of his windbreaker and said, 'Here. Shoot some of the bastards before you surrender.' Dietrich thought he was wonderful.

So they sallied forth to entertain the troops. Marlene sang a few songs, cracked a few jokes, stalked around in her gold dress, giving the sex-starved GIs full benefit of her figure, thanks to the painful body stocking.

And then she came to the highpoint of her act. Sitting straddled on a chair with her legs widespread, she began to play a tune in her musical saw. She wasn't particularly good, but that didn't matter to the gawping GIs squatting on the ground below the improvised stage. For they could see right up the famous film star's crotch. It was something they would be able to boast about for a long time.

But this tour would be shortlived as far as Patton's forward areas were concerned. Bing Crosby and Dinah Shore were fifteen minutes into their concert with men of the 79th Infantry Division when the balloon went up on the evening of 18 September. The day before they had taken the surrender of a whole German motorized regiment under the command of a Colonel Wetzel, who had taken out his glass eye and placed it on the table as he discussed terms with the Americans. Now the infantrymen were pleased with themselves, glad to relax and enjoy this brief respite from combat. But it wasn't to be. Suddenly the public address system started reading out a long list of combat teams who were to return to their outfits immediately. Bing Crosby stood on the stage, smiling a little helplessly. Rapidly the hall emptied, leaving the USO show with only a handful of spectators. Bing threw up his hands in despair. It was the same everywhere along the Third Army's front. The Germans were attacking again in strength. There was no time now for Marlene or Bing.

*　　*　　*

Gentleman jockey General Hasso von Manteuffel, the commander of the German Fifth Panzer Army, was not particularly happy with the strength of his assault force. It consisted of two panzer divisions, three panzer brigades, plus supporting infantry from a panzer grenadier division, grouped in two corps. On paper the force looked formidable. But several of the armoured units didn't have their full complement of tanks and his 11th Panzer Division, coming up from the south, where it had dodged all attempts by the US 7th Army to destroy it, had not yet arrived in the battle area.

Still the little ex-cavalryman, who had risen from regimental to army commander in four years, was determined to do his utmost. The knowledge that the plan of attack had come from Hitler steeled his determination. These days Hitler was having generals who he felt had failed shot.

In essence, the plan envisaged the Fifth Panzer Army striking Patton's 4th Armored Division in the flank, retaking the town of Luneville and wiping out the American bridgeheads on the Moselle. Hitler wanted to destroy the threat posed to the Siegfried Line by Patton's offensive, which had started two days before, so that he could concentrate on the great attack soon to come through the Ardennes.

*　　*　　*

Now as the German panzers rolled towards the coming battle, their artillery already softening up the enemy positions, the Gestapo and their French agents made one last determined effort to wipe out Franks's SAS and the loyal Frenchmen who helped them. With luck von Manteuffel's attack would be a success and the German police authorities didn't want the SAS and their Maquis followers reporting von Manteuffel's movements back to Allied intelligence.

Aided by SS troopers, the Gestapo swooped on the little village of Moussey, where Franks's 2nd SAS Regiment had been loyally supported by most of the villagers. Again informers had related to the Gestapo what the people of Moussey had done for the SAS. As Lieutenant Christopher Sykes, who was one of the SAS survivors, wrote after the war, 'We depended upon the people of Moussey for many of the necessities of life and for help of every kind. It was a nightmare time but throughout it the civilian population were in far greater danger than we were.'

Now, with threats and blows from their rifle butts, the women weeping and the children screaming, the Gestapo and SS rounded up the whole male population of Moussey in the village square. Bravely the village priest, Abbé Moliere, offered his own life in exchange for those of the men. The Gestapo told him to mind his own business and stay with the women. Thereupon 256 men were taken away, first to the only concentration camp on French soil, Struthof-Natzweiler, and from there to Dachau and Belsen. Finally they were sent to the extermination camp at Auschwitz. Of the 256 who were marched away that grim September day only 144 returned. It was no different at the other small towns and villages in which the SAS had received assistance. Senones had 350 deported, of whom 235 died. La Petite Raon, one of the SAS's first objectives, lost 128 out of 193 deportees. Three villages were burned to the ground and twenty-nine Frenchmen were shot on the spot.

The massive attack which coincided with von Manteuffel's thrust put an end to the Maquis in those quiet hills. Sadly Colonel Franks thought it was time to smuggle his survivors through the German lines to the US 7th Army. Behind him he left thirty-nine of his troopers unaccounted for.

*　　*　　*

The main thrust of von Manteuffel's attack came in and around Luneville. It was confused and bitter, with Sherman tanks stalking the enemy Panthers through the debris-littered streets. Under the impact of the gunfire, houses trembled like stage drops. There were fires everywhere and both sides made full use of their anti-tank rockets as the infantry made short work of any tank caught off guard.

In the fog and rain Allied air superiority was of little use. So it was man against man, with Patton's favourite division, the Fourth Armored, commanded by General Wood, giving as good as it took.

Von Manteuffel threw in everything he had, one panzer division, two other armoured brigades and a panzer grenadier division. But Wood's Fourth held them off, though the enemy's tanks were far superior to those of the Americans. Losses mounted on both sides. But in the midst of the blood and brutality there were moments of grim humour.

Nat Fraenkel, an ex-New York cab driver, was rolling forward in his Sherman when he saw a German tank 'pivoting not thirty yards in front of me. I fired three shots at it, figuring to force it backwards. All three shots bounded harmlessly off the side. What do I see but a German officer stick his head out of the turret and smile at me! He then proceeded to pull a white handkerchief out of his pocket and wipe it against the side of his machine where my bullets had marked it. He smiled again as if to forgive me for scratching his property; then he put the handkerchief back in his pocket!'

Even against the grim background of the military hospitals behind the front in Verdun and Nancy a kind of humour persisted. Young Lieutenant Erich Huett had been wounded by the Maquis and then handed over to the Americans, who were now tending his wounds in Verdun. Unfortunately, or so he thought, Huett belonged to the 17 SS Panzergrenadier Division. At first he was taken to task by the senior nursing sister, a major named Helen, who asked him if he wasn't ashamed of being looked after by a Jewish Nurse when he himself had probably killed lots of Jews. But Huett was young, blond and handsome and Helen seemed to take a liking to him. Every time she came to visit, not only would she examine him but would also slide her hand under the sheets and leave a packet of cigarettes on his naked belly before checking that 'I really was a male'.

When Huett told the other patients what had happened they were jealous. One said, 'I'm going to learn English too.' A wounded artillery captain threatened, after Huett had distributed the cigarettes, 'You keep it up. Otherwise you're going to be in trouble with us lot.' Huett kept

1. 'Colonel Brian Franks, a veteran of the war in the shadows in North Africa, Sicily and Italy' (p.3).

2. 'Colonel Blair Mayne, known to his men simply as "Colonel Paddy"' (p.5).

3/4. 'Patton was almost pathologically anti-British, focusing his hatred on Montgomery...' (p.24).

5. 'Marlene Dietrich was in business. In a moment she could go out and entertain the troops of Patton's Third Army' (p.47).

'The best publicist of all for the Fourth Infantry Division... Ernest Hemingway' (p.33).

7. American medics gather up the wounded after the crossing of the River Moselle (see pp.20-22).

8. The railway bridge over the River Saar at Saarguemines destroyed by the retreating Germans.

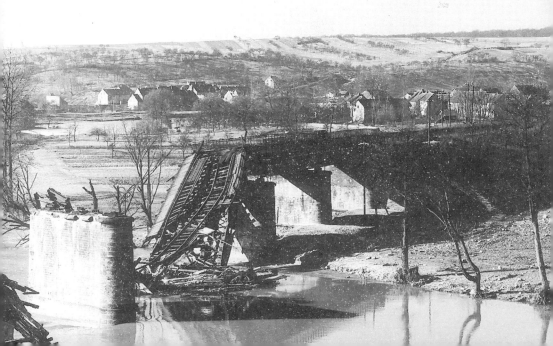

it up in both senses of the word and continued to receive gifts of cigarettes and chocolate from Major Helen 'after the obligatory touch under
the sheet' until at last he was healthy enough to be sent to a POW camp.

But the battle still raged in and around Luneville. On the morning of
the 19th forty German Panthers and Mark IVs came racing out of the
mist to attack the Fourth Division. As the divisional historian wrote,
'When you stand by a wide-tracked Panther, it looks as big as a house
and the barrel of its high velocity gun seems to run out for miles.' But
they were stopped by the tank destroyers of the 10th, 35th and 696th
Field Artillery Battalions.

In some cases, blinded by the mist and driving rain, the American tank
destroyers got within fifty yards of the advancing German tanks. But the
pressure was starting to tell. Patton threw in his other veteran armoured
division, the Sixth, which, like the Fourth, had been fighting since the
first of August.

General Gerow, its commander, had come to see Patton on 17
September and Patton had told him that he thought his Sixth Division
might be transferred to Hodges' 1st Army to support Montgomery in
the north. Gerow had better get himself involved in a battle if he didn't
want that to happen. Now Gerow had his battle, as von Manteuffel
stepped up the pressure and one of the biggest tank battles of the whole
campaign raged.

On the 20th the German Army Group G Commander was relieved
on Hitler's express order. He was replaced by General Balck, who had
been wounded six times in battle in two wars and was regarded as a
fervent Nazi; his way of punishing officers who failed in their missions
was to have them shot. Two days before, Balck had been interviewed
by Hitler on his way from the East to the new front in Lorraine. There
he had been subjected to a long harangue on the military situation in the
West. The Führer had informed him that, due to supply difficulties, the
Anglo–American advance was bound to come to a halt on a line running
from the mouth of the Scheldt along the line of the West Wall to Metz
and from there to the Vosges.

Then Hitler had let Balck into the great secret. Once the Allies had
been brought to a halt, he would attack in the Ardennes, probably some
time in mid-November.

Balck was shocked by the thought of Germany going over to the
offensive so soon after the great defeat in the West, but, good Nazi that
he was, he knew that Hitler was telling the truth.

Finally Hitler gave him his final orders. He was to hold Alsace-

Lorraine at all costs; the political situation in Germany at that moment demanded that the two old Imperial provinces should be retained. It would also be his job to fight for time. On no account must he allow a situation to develop in which the forces now being earmarked for the Ardennes offensive would have to be sidetracked to Army Group G.

This, then, was the officer who Hitler had appointed to stop Patch's Seventh Army and Patton's Third. He was arrogant, aggressive and ruthless. He was, in short, the kind of commander in whom Hitler felt confidence. If anyone could stop Patton, it would be *General der Panzertruppe* Hermann Balck.

★   ★   ★

The second week of September gave way to the third. The fighting still raged, but Luneville had been cleared and it seemed as if the steam had gone out of the German attack. Still Patton's men were making no headway at Metz. The city stubbornly refused to surrender as it had done to the Germans back in 1870.

Angrily Patton went out to visit a regiment of the 90th Infantry Division, not one of his favourite divisions, in the line between Metz and Thionville. Both he and his aide, Colonel Codman, knew the terrain well. They had been there a quarter of a century ago and, as Codman noted in a letter home, 'The houses, inhabitants, chickens and manure piles look and smell exactly as they did then.'

The regiment that Patton was visiting was stretched paper-thin. Sergeant Mims, his driver, started to get apprehensive. They were too close to the front and he didn't want to drive the Army Commander into the German lines. He began to slow down.

'Keep going,' Patton ordered. Mims did, until at last Patton told him to stop; it was now clear to the equally apprehensive Codman that 'we were well out in front of everything'.

Patton swept his front with his field glasses and remarked to Codman after a while, 'I feel rather like Marshal Ney. I don't remember what battle, but at a critical moment Napoleon, riding across country, comes across the Marshal wandering about by himself with a rifle on his shoulder. "Is your rearguard adequate?" The Emperor asks. "Quite adequate," Ney replies. "I am the rearguard."'

Moments later Patton ordered Mims to drive to the rear. As Codman wrote, 'Nothing happened.' For the General it was a disappointment.

Codman knew that Patton often took calculated risks to impress his men. He wanted to show them that the Commanding General was also prepared to take the risks they did. But was he courting death this day? Codman had often heard him say that he hoped for 'a quick and pain-less death inflicted by the last bullet of the last battle'.

But Codman also knew that this wasn't the last battle by a long way. 'He will be there pitching to the bitter end; so why risk being shot by some stray German rifleman on this cold wet September day in Lorraine? Was it, Codman wondered, because he felt he had no control of the events to come. As Codman wrote, 'These are the corroding thoughts to which the General finds an antidote in an occasional roll of the dice with fate. In all probability he will be held in leash. If so, there will be strange and costly reprisals. Then, as usual, General Patton will be called in to save the critical day.'

Strangely prophetic words, written on 25 September 1944, three months before the launching of the Ardennes offensive in which Patton did exactly that, and on the same day that Hitler laid the foundations for the great 'surprise' attack! For, on the same day the Führer commanded Jodl to draw up a comprehensive plan for the offensive. To Keitel he assigned the task of calculating what ammunition and supplies would be required and when they could be delivered. Furthermore he ordered five panzer divisions to be withdrawn from the front and brought to the Cologne area for re-training and re-organization. These five divisions would form the backbone of what the Germans would later call the 'Rundstedt Offensive'.

Romantic that he was, Patton believed he possessed second sight. Had he, on that September day, some sort of foresight of what was to come? *Or had he reached certain conclusions from the evidence now provided for him by von Manteuffel's 'surprise' counter-attack in the Luneville-Nancy region?*

7

BLOODY AACHEN

Nearly two weeks before Patton had driven to the front and had seemingly dared the Germans to kill him, the Japanese Ambassador in Berlin had had a long conversation with Hitler. 58-year old Baron Oshima, a soldier and an aristocrat, had first come to Berlin as the Japanese military attaché in 1934. Here he had forged excellent contacts with the German military, leading industrialists and the heads of the National Socialist Party, a party which he greatly admired. In 1939 he had been recalled to Tokyo for a year, returning in 1940 as Japanese Ambassador. Thus he became Tokyo's representative in the 'Pact of Steel' (Germany, Italy and Japan). He was a man to whom all doors were open.

While Oshima was in Japan in 1939, the US Signal Intelligence Service had broken the Japanese Diplomatic code, an operation known as 'MAGIC'. From now until the end of the war, the Americans and the British were able to read all Oshima's coded signals from Berlin in what was known as the 'Black Ultra', due to the fact that the decodes were given to their various recipients in black folders. Thus, when Ultra, the British de-coding operation run from Bletchley in Buckinghamshire wasn't working, Magic was. Among other things, it provided the Western Allies with a major insight into Hitler's thinking and intentions. Indeed General Marshall, Eisenhower's boss in Washington, maintained that 'The conduct of General Eisenhower's campaign and of all the operations in the Pacific are closely related in conception and timing to the information we secretly obtain through these intercepted codes. They contribute greatly to the victory and tremendously to the saving of American lives.'

Time and again the Oshima decodes had been proved right. Now on 6 September, after his meeting with Hitler, he sent the following record of what Hitler had said to him to Tokyo: 'In an area such as France, where there are good roads, once the German lines had been breached by a large task force, it was necessary to fall back to new positions. Accordingly it was determined to withdraw most of the forces to the West Wall, even from the Antwerp area, leaving behind garrison troops in the most important coastal fortifications such as Bordeaux, Le Havre and the Brittany ports . . .'From the beginning we have realized that in order to stabilize our lines it would be necessary to launch a German counter-attack. Accordingly troops are now being massed south-east of Nancy with the intention of striking from the flank at the American forces on the south-east wing which have been pursuing us in five or six columns, each composed of three or four divisions.'

Hitler went on to tell Oshima: 'In that attack it is planned to employ Army Group G commanded by *Generaloberst* Blaskowitz and also troops moved up from Germany itself. Except for small security detachments operating on the banks of the Loire and rearguard units in the area of the Rhône River, the main strength of Blaskowitz's Army Group is falling back to a planned line without suffering serious losses . . .'

Then Hitler said, 'The offensive I have just mentioned will be only for the purpose of stabilizing the present front. However, when the current replenishment of the air forces is completed and when the new army of more than a million men which is now being organized is ready, I intend to combine the new units with units to be withdrawn from all possible areas and to open a large-scale offensive in the West.'

Oshima reported to Tokyo that he then asked Hitler when this major offensive would be launched.

'At the beginning of November,' Hitler replied. 'We will be assisted in holding off the enemy during September and October by the comparatively rainy weather that will restrict the enemy's employment of their superior airpower.'

Oshima then remarked, according to the decode, that he was worried that the Third Reich might not be able to hold the line in the West until Germany was in a position to launch the great offensive. He was worried, too, about the delay in the attack which would be caused by the time it took to organize the new army and equip it.

'I have complete confidence in the West Wall,' Hitler answered. 'Furthermore, even though [words missing in the decode] the line may require some withdrawal I expect that for the most part we shall be able to maintain it. As for our ability to organize and equip new troops, I do not believe there will be any difficulty, in view of the efforts of Speer.*

In his message to Tokyo Oshima summed up his thinking after the meeting. He reported that 'Hitler's decision to conduct a general mobilization and then to launch a great offensive on the Western Front with troops drawn from all possible areas is, in my opinion, the correct step for Germany to take in the present situation. Furthermore if Japan can bring about a Russo-German peace before the time set for such an offensive, Germany would, without a doubt, be able to achieve a decisive and imposing victory on the Western Front.'

Eisenhower read this top-level 'Black Ultra' intelligence that September. Probably he passed on the information about the counter-attack to be launched in Lorraine by the German Army Group G. Now he and Patton had confirmation of the veracity of the Oshima decode. The Germans *had* attacked in exactly the area mentioned by Hitler.

The question still remains as to why Eisenhower did not take any action on the vital secret which Hitler revealed to the Japanese Ambassador, namely that Hitler was playing for time until he could launch his offensive in the West. Nor did he follow up the warnings of an impending German attack in the West given by further Oshima decodes in October and November.

Was it because Baron Oshima always expressed his own doubts about German capabilities in his summaries of his conversations with Hitler and later the German Foreign Minister, von Ribbentrop? Was it because, although he knew that the Germans *were* going to attack (he admitted as much to the US Secretary of War, Patterson, a year later) he didn't know *where*? Was it because, due to his 'Broad Front Strategy', he couldn't concentrate his troops anywhere on the 500-mile front, save where he was attacking?

Or was it something else? How, otherwise, could one take Colonel Codman's strangely prophetic statement that September afternoon about General Patton being called upon 'to save the critical day'.

So many questions with so few answers.** But one thing Eisenhower must have realized when he read that Oshima decode of 6 September: the Germans were determined to hold the West Wall until the great new army Hitler had promised them was ready. If Germany was going to be defeated in 1944, the Western Allies would soon have to break through

---

* Minister of Armament and War Production.
** For further discussion of this question see C. Whiting: *The Last Assault*, (Leo Cooper Ltd).

that last defence line behind which the new army was being assembled. It was imperative that Eisenhower's armies broke through *now*. But where?

★ ★ ★

Two days before Patton's attack on the Siegfried Line had been stalled by the German counter-attack at Luneville, General Hodges, the commander of the US 1st Army, decided to have another crack at the Siegfried Line. (His V Corps which had led the first assault still held their positions in the Line, but not for long.) The place he picked was the area of the old German border city of Aachen.

It seemed to most observers to be the most unlikely place for the Americans to achieve any success. Back in 1938 the builders of the West Wall had ensured that the city, in which Charlemagne was buried, was defended more strongly than any other city close to the frontier. They erected two lines of fortifications about five miles apart. The first band, called the Scharnhorst Line after the famous German commander of the Napoleonic wars, ran along the frontier with Holland and Belgium. The second, even stronger and thicker, was called the Schill Line and covered the two 'corridors' made up of the small towns of Stolberg and Monschau.

But the Corps Commander to whom Hodges gave the task of breaking through these formidable fortifications was confident he could do it. General 'Lightning Joe' Collins, commander of Hodges' VII Corps, who looked ten years younger than his 47 years and who was Hodges' favourite general (as he was Montgomery's favourite US one), was not interested in the old imperial city. All he wanted was to break the defences around Aachen and rush for the Rhine some forty miles away.

For this task he summoned two experienced and reliable divisions, his First, 'the Big Red One', and General Rose's Third Armored, the 'Spearhead Division', as it called itself proudly. The Third, commanded by General Maurice Rose, who had risen to general's rank in a prejudiced US Regular Army in spite of being a rabbi's son, was only a thousand yards away from the Siegfried Line. All the same Rose, a cavalryman who had been trained by Patton, an anti-Semite, and who had a reputation for being a strict disciplinarian – he was always threatening his officers with a court-martial – still expected a lot of trouble in breaking through. The General, who was killed in action a month before the war ended, knew the Germans would 'fight like the devil' in order to save Aachen. Still, like General Huebner, commanding the 1st

57

Infantry who, like he, had risen from private to general officer in a long career in the Army, he knew that orders were orders. So he prepared to kick off his advance on the morning of 14 September.

Unknown to the two generals and to their Corps Commander 'Lightning Joe', everything was in the attackers' favour that night before the assault. In Aachen panic and confusion reigned after dark that evening. On the orders, and the threats, of the Nazi Party bosses, the Aacheners were evacuating the city. With them went deserters and reluctant heroes, trying to get out of Aachen before it was too late, plus those same Party officials who had ordered that Aachen should be defended to the 'last round and the last man'.

That evening General Count von Schwerin, who commanded the 116th Panzer Division which was to defend the city, drove past long columns of old men, women and children, their carts piled high with their pathetic bits and pieces. The aristocratic general didn't like what he saw. He frowned and drove into his HQ, Aachen's top hotel, *Der Quellenhof*, which boasted a Roman bath, and asked himself in the light of what he had just seen what he should do.

The man who commanded the 'Greyhound Division', as the 116th Panzer was called, was remarkably like the man who a dozen miles away was planning to attack the line at Aachen. Both had the same high forehead, the slicked-down hair and the pugnacious jaw. Von Schwerin could have been 'Lightning Joe's' big brother. But the German general, whom Hitler thought was 'a splendid battlefield commander' but who 'unfortunately is not a National Socialist', was not feeling particularly brotherly that evening. Indeed he felt decidedly angry. The local Party bosses had fled, leaving the city to its fate.

'With what' von Schwerin asked his staff, 'am I supposed to fight to the last round and the last man?'

Apart from his own battered panzer division, the defenders of Aachen consisted of a 'stomach and eye battalion', some Hitler Youth and whatever stragglers had not managed to escape from the traps set up by the military police around the beleagured city.

'A lot of Christmas tree soldiers,' von Schwerin snorted. He made his decision on the spot. He would take the crack 116th Panzer and fight north of the city. Aachen would be left to the *Amis*.

Now the 'Big Red One' started to fire on the city, living up to their reputation of being the first to do everything. In the First World War they had been the first to fire at the Germans and they had fired the first shots of the US Army in the Second World War in Africa. Now they

58

were the first to fire into Germany. As their shells started to land on the crossroads at Bildchen, von Schwerin scribbled a hasty note in English for the *Amis* soon to come, as he thought. It read: 'I stopped the absurd evacuation of this town; therefore I am responsible for the fate of its inhabitants and I ask you in the case of an occupation by your troops to take care of the unfortunate population in a humane way. I am the last Commanding Officer in the Sector of Aachen. Schwerin.'*

Von Schwerin handed the note to an employee of Aachen's main post office, telling him to give it to the first American officer entering the city. Even as he did so he realized that he had virtually signed his own death warrant. If things went wrong Hitler would have no hesitation in having him strangled with chicken wire, as he had done with those generals who had taken part in the July assassination plot against him; and von Schwerin knew he was already under suspicion on that account.

Then he was on his way with his battered division. Collins had been handed Aachen together with the Scharnhorst Line part of the West Wall, on a platter.

★   ★   ★

On 13 September the 3rd Armored Division's Task Force X, led by a colonel with the heroic name of Leander, Lieutenant-Colonel Leander Doan to be exact, had discovered a small cart track leading through the Scharnhorst Line. In the four years since the Germans had vacated the Line a farmer had built this small track through the dragon's teeth covering the pillboxes as a short cut for his cattle. Now Rose ordered Doan to advance along the track, though it was blocked by a 'flail'.**

But first the flail tank had to be removed. Thus Sergeant Dahl and his platoon commander, Lieutenant John Hoffmann, found themselves directly in front of the Siegfried Line pillboxes, sweating furiously as they tried to tow the crippled flail away and make room for Doan's column to advance.

Not that Colonel Doan was very sanguine about his chances. Darkness was approaching and at night the Sherman, with its high silhouette, was very vulnerable. Even a 'Christmas tree soldier', armed with the throw-away German rocket–launcher *der Panzerfaust*, could knock out 20,000 dollars of expensive machinery, and with it a highly trained crew of

---

* That note is still preserved in Aachen.
** A British-invented device: a Sherman tank equipped with steel chains, the flail, to detonate mines in its path.

specialists, with little risk to himself. Still Doan knew that Rose was not a man to be crossed. His orders had to be obeyed. So Doan's Shermans started to clank down the cart track one by one until twenty of them had vanished into the September gloom, heading straight for the West Wall.

What happened next Doan had feared and expected all along. On both sides of the cart track German soldiers sprang up, long tubes on their right shoulder. A dry crack, a spurt of yellow flame, then the first pot-shaped projectile was hurrying towards the Shermans, trailing red sparks behind it. A hollow boom, a moment's glow of superheated metal, a thick crump and the stricken Sherman lurched to a halt.

In the next five minutes Doan lost four tanks to the German infantry. Perched high on the track, the Shermans were sitting ducks. There was no room to manoeuvre. Now the track was filled with his tankers running for their lives, as they were pursued by the tracer of the German machine guns.

There was worse to come. To the right of the stalled column there came the rumble of heavy tracks. It had to be the enemy. There were no friendly tanks ahead. Before Doan could make up his mind whether he should retreat or not the first Ferdinand self-propelled guns of the German 34th Assault Gun Brigade loomed up out of the night.

The Ferdinands' 90mm guns thundered. Number Five Sherman trembled violently and started to burn. Doan was virtually powerless against the new attackers. The Germans easily outgunned the Shermans and the Ferdinands' armour-piercing shells were much superior to the Shermans' solid shot. Helplessly he watched as the assault guns turned his column into a charnel house. One after another six more of his remaining sixteen Shermans were picked off.

Doan gave in. Within an hour he had lost half his command. The Third Division's first attempt to break through the West Wall had failed badly. He gave the order to dig in. To his front the ten lost Shermans continued to burn.

★   ★   ★

Now it was the turn of the 'Big Red One'. They launched their attack on 14 September, with surprising success. They went straight through the first line of pillboxes and the regiment concerned, the 16th Infantry, reported to HQ that the German defences were hardly worthy of the name. The boastful men of America's premier division pressed on glee-fully, advancing deeper and on a broad front through the Siegfried Line. By nightfall on the next day they had completed their mission. They had breached the Scharnhorst Line and Aachen was surrounded on three sides. Now it was up to Rose's 3rd Armored to do the rest.

But on that Friday morning when the 'Spearhead Division' took up the challenge once more things were beginning to change in Aachen. It was over fifty hours since von Schwerin had scribbled that fatal note, virtually declaring Aachen an open city, and the *Amis* had still not arrived. Von Schwerin was a brave man; he had been wounded several times during the last years and had won all Germany's top awards for gallantry in the field. Still, he didn't want to end up in the Gestapo's cellars. So he rescinded his order. But already it was too late. His note had been discovered by Party officials who had returned to the beleaguered city.

On that Friday morning, as Rose's tankers attacked again, von Schwerin received a call from his corps commander, General Schack.

'Schwerin,' the Corps Commander told him somewhat sadly, 'it can be only a matter of hours now before you are relieved of your command. Place yourself at my disposal please.' Without another word Schack hung up.

Now von Schwerin brooded in his isolated farmhouse HQ, not knowing what to do. But already Hitler had ordered from his Eastern HQ that he should be court-martialled and a full SS General, *Standartenführer* Przybiksi, was on his way to bring back von Schwerin 'dead or alive'.

* * *

Even as von Schwerin was taking that fateful phone call, Rose's 3rd Armored had started its attack on the Siegfried Line. In the lead in the assault on the Schill Line was the task force commanded by Colonel Loveday. The Colonel's name may have made him sound a little romantic. In fact he was a hard-driving officer who urged his combat command forward and pressed the 'Christmas Tree soldiers' back relentlessly, heading hell-for-leather for the Schill Line. Nothing could stop him, it seemed.

During the night of Friday 15 September the third-rate German soldiers melted away in front of Loveday. He captured the first line of bunkers. As soon as it was dawn the Americans pushed on again past empty pillboxes, their guns unmanned. Ahead lay open country. The task force was through the West Wall!

Now Loveday's point advanced between the two villages of Mausbach and Gressenich, both lying in a shallow valley bordered by wooded heights, an ideal position for an ambush. Loveday's tankers were confident but cautious. Radios hummed as they kept in contact with one another. They rode with their turret hatches 'buttoned up', searching the ground ahead and the two flanks as best they could through their calibrated glass periscopes. Were they riding into a trap? It all looked too easy. The first line of Shermans reached the half-way point between the white-painted houses. There was no sign of life. Had the Krauts abandoned the villages as well? They rumbled on.

Then from both flanks came the white blobs of AP shells. Squat German Mark IV tanks and great lumbering SP guns were coming out of their hiding places. A series of hollow booms. A Sherman reeled back on its bogies. Another rolled to a halt, a gleaming silver hole skewered in its side. Frantically the crews baled out and pelted to the rear through the smoke. A boxlike US ambulance, its red crosses clearly visible, bounced out to meet them. The German gunners didn't hesitate. A sharp crack and the ambulance disappeared momentarily in a ball of smoke and flame. When it had cleared there were dead and dying men sprawled everywhere.

With seven Shermans and one tank destroyer knocked out in short order, Loveday had had enough. He radioed General Rose for permission to pull back to Mausbach. Reluctantly Rose gave permission when he learned that Loveday had less than forty per cent of his effectives left. The 'Spearhead Division' had finally done what 'Lightning Joe' had requested. They had broken through and now the ring around Aachen was almost complete.

But on that same Saturday night when Loveday pulled back, General Eric Brandenburger, the pedantic commander of the German 7th Army, issued the following order: 'The Seventh Army will defend its position . . . and the West Wall to the last man and the last bullet. The penetrations achieved by the enemy will be recaptured. The forward line of bunkers will be regained.' The real battle was about to begin.

8

THE LULL

That Saturday, some fifty miles away, General Gerow's Fifth Armored Division, which still maintained V Corps' bridgehead over the River Sauer and through the Siegfried Line, came under attack. Field Marshal von Rundstedt, Germany's greatest soldier, had helped to plan the German attack personally, for he saw the danger of what was called the 'Wallendorf Bridgehead'.

Just after dark a newly arrived German flak regiment opened up with its anti-aircraft guns. The gunners used their air bursts on the American battalion at the village of Wettingen to deadly effect. Men went down everywhere as the fist-sized chunks of glowing shrapnel hissed lethally through the air above their foxholes. As the official US history of the campaign states, the battalion suffered 'almost overwhelming casualties'. Still the battalion, sadly depleted now and forced to keep cover most of the time, not venturing out of their foxholes even to carry out their bodily functions, held on.

On the morning of the 17th the order was given for the battered battalion to pull back. So a very difficult manoeuvre began – the Americans withdrawing and the Germans attacking, in this case with the armour of a once crack *Panzerlehrdivision* (The German Army's demonstration division for armour) and the paras of the 3rd Parachute Division. They struck the hard-pressed Americans at several points of the eastern tip of the salient. Still, three and a half hours after the attack had begun, the defenders could report to HQ that they had the situation in hand. They had knocked out eight German tanks and killed several score of their infantry.

Von Rundstedt was angry. The old fox, who had never lost a battle yet, thought the paras and the tankers had attacked at the wrong spot. They should have hit the base of the salient near Wallendorf, not the tip.

On the 19th an all-out attack, carried out by the 19th *Volksgrenadierdivision*, was launched at the southern flank of the bridge-head. The young grenadiers pushed forward rapidly, reaching the other end of the two bridges which the Americans had thrown over the Sauer.

General Oliver, commanding the 5th Armored Division, was pleased with the efforts of his defenders after a near panic two days before when some of his men had fled. All the same he thought he could improve his position by reducing the length of his perimeter. He ordered his men to withdraw again to the high ground near Wallendorf. There they were to hold the new position 'until corps permits withdrawal'.

Seeing the *Amis* moving back, the triumphant Germans redoubled their efforts. Heavy shelling and relentless attacks on the two bridges followed. Still the tankers and the armored infantry held on.

Late that afternoon Corps HQ gave permission to withdraw and the bridgehead was abandoned. That was the end of V Corps' attempts to penetrate the Siegfried Line and drive to the Rhine. Now nothing much would happen in the Eifel-Ardennes for the next three months. When the fighting did flare up again on this remote front on 16 December 1944, it would shock the western world.

★ ★ ★

That Saturday the 'Wild Buffaloes' started to unload from the transports to tackle Collins' VII Corps. The 'Wild Buffaloes' were the soldiers of the 12th Infantry Division. It had gained its nickname back in 1941 in Russia when it had driven to the River Volga, 'sweeping everything in front of it like a heard of wild buffaloes'. Three years later, although the divisional sign was still a raging buffalo tearing down a fence, the old fire had gone. There were few of the old Buffaloes left. Now the Division's ranks were filled with young and inexperienced soldiers, though under the German system, as always, there were cadres of experienced NCOs and officers to lead the new boys.

Moreover, the Division was commanded by Colonel Engel, 36 years old, ardent and arrogant. He had once been Hitler's adjutant and had asked the Führer personally for a combat command. As Colonel von Gersdorff of the German Seventh Army noted, 'He was probably on the phone to Hitler all the time'. Now this fervent Nazi was going to lead his new division against the *Amis*, commanded by the son of a poor Eastern European Rabbi.

As the fog started to sweep in, the Buffaloes came straight from their railheads and headed for their confrontation with Rose's tankmen of the 'Spearhead Division'.

The German attackers' orders were stark and simple – and brutal. They were to drive forward in a two-pronged thrust, fling the *Amis* out of their positions and restore the Schill Line. The West Wall had to be retaken *at all costs*. The German guns opened up with a hoarse scream. The silence was ripped apart by the shells hissing towards the Third Division's positions. Immediately the leading American infantry went to ground as the very earth trembled. The German multiple mortars joined in, sending six-pronged stabs of red flame into the sky.

Hardly had the barrage begun to die away, leaving the waiting GIs ashen-faced and shocked, than the young men of the 27th Fusilier Regiment of the 12th Infantry came charging the American positions, their bayonets fixed, in disciplined waves, as if they were on some peace-time training ground.

The GIs forgot their shock. This was an ideal target. Whistles shrilled. NCOs bellowed orders. Radios crackled. The GIs began to pop their helmeted heads above the rims of their foxholes and prepared to fire at the grey-uniformed figures running towards them.

Far to the rear, in some cases five miles, the artillery took up the challenge. Closer to the front the heavy 4.2 mortars cracked into action. Shells started to explode among the attacking Germans. Great brown holes appeared like the work of gigantic moles. Gaps appeared in the ranks of the charging men. But still they came on.

Perhaps a couple of dozen reached the American line. None crossed it. In the open they had left scores of their comrades. Little groups who had managed to save themselves cowered in holes or gullies while the American machine guns swept the fields.

Again they came on in a new assault. But they could not break the American resistance. In the end they pulled back, ignoring the threats of the handful of officers and NCOs who had survived the mass murder. Behind them they left their dead sprawled out in the fields. The total cost to the defenders – two dead and twenty-two wounded.

★   ★   ★

It was no different for Colonel Engel's other formation, the 48th Grenadier Regiment. The defenders stopped their assault dead. What was left of them was then pounded by American artillery. It wasn't war; it was slaughter. When the smoke from the artillery bombardment cleared away to reveal the stark brutality of those killing fields even the most hard-bitten of the American observers were shocked. Later, American observers estimated that, of the first two assault companies, perhaps some 250 riflemen in all, only ten had escaped.

Thrown in piecemeal, without proper reconnaissance and knowledge of the terrain, Engel's men had paid a terrible price for their commander's overweening ambition to prove himself as a divisional commander.* Indeed Hitler's former adjutant was forced to ask the despised *Amis* for a truce to collect his dead.

Such truces were specifically forbidden by the Führer, but as Engel had Hitler's ear he could afford to disobey him. In the same manner he called off a further attack scheduled for the following day. The Chief-of-Staff of the German Seventh Army, Colonel von Gersdorff, was sent to remonstrate with him on this score and found him drinking coffee and eating cake and whipped cream while outside American shells came whizzing down.

'Where's the cellar?' von Gersdorff asked anxiously.

Engel laughed and answered, 'The *Amis* always shoot at the same target. There's no danger from the Americans unless their gun-layer makes a mistake.'

So the two senior officers sat together, eating cake and cream, while outside the little forward CP the mud-splattered ambulances rumbled by, bearing their cargoes of broken-limbed young men.

★   ★   ★

The Buffaloes' attack was a bloody failure, but the appearance of this new full scale division – it had 15,000 men – and the other new formations that von Rundstedt was pumping into the Siegfried Line around Aachen and elsewhere created the effect the aged Field Marshal desired. They convinced Collins, just as they had his fellow Corps Commander, Gerow, that he wasn't going to succeed in breaking through the West Wall in depth this September. 'A combination of things stopped us,' Collins recalled later. 'We ran out of gas – that is to say we weren't completely dry, but the effect was much the same – we ran out of ammunition and we ran out of weather. The loss of our close tactical air support because of the weather was a real blow.'

But the attackers had also run out of steam.

After the war the US commanders all put forward the same argument.

---

* The Colonel, who was later promoted general, lived to become an old man and die peacefully in bed.

They hadn't the supplies to continue the attacks, for naturally those supplies had gone to Montgomery. But if they hadn't the supplies, why had they attacked in the first place? After all they were all confident that they were going to be able to drive right to the Rhine. And to drive to the Rhine they would need far more in the way of supplies than they would just to breach the Siegfried Line.

In the tank and rifle companies which really did the fighting losses had been high and the enemy held, as Collins himself admitted, 'really beautiful positions'. Behind the lines the little field hospitals at Eupen, Verviers, St Vith and the bigger one at Liège were filling up with young men suffering from gunshot wounds, but not only from wounds. There were hundreds, later thousands, who had come down with chest complaints, combat exhaustion and trenchfoot, lying on their beds with their swollen toes exposed, wads of iodine-soaked cottonwool between each sausage-like member, each hoping that he wouldn't have to have his feet amputated.

The cost of the First Army's first 'reconnaissance in force', as it was called, had been high – some 10,000 casualties of all kinds. All the same as the end of September approached and there was a lull in the fighting in Hodges' sector, the initial disappointment at this failure to break through the West Wall was slowly replaced by a new optimism. From divisional headquarters close to the front to Hodges' own way back at Spa the staff officers told each other they'd do it next time. As soon as they had all the gas, all the ammo and all the replacement 'doughs', they'd break through and drive for the Rhine.

Little did these confident planners know that it would cost the US Army 130,000 casualties (79,000 battle and 51,000 non-battle) – more than the total for the whole Vietnam War – to fight the Battle of the West Wall over the next three months. By the time December arrived many of those planners would have lost their confidence and secretly believe that the Wall was impregnable.

★   ★   ★

Now it was nearly winter. The wooded ridges of the Eifel–Ardennes were constantly wreathed in mists. Often a cold drizzle fell, the raindrops dripping mournfully from the firs. Mostly that was the only sound, for the fighting had ceased save to the north where Hodges' 30th Infantry Division were still trying to break through at Aachen and to the south where Patton despaired of ever taking Metz.

Tours 'in the line' were reminiscent of those quiet periods in the trenches in the First World War. Future military historian Captain Charles MacDonald recalled after the war 'going up' with his company of the 2nd Infantry Division. Leaving the last Belgian village of Schoenberg, his truck convoy wound its way up the steep hill to Germany. 'A big white signboard with glaring letters told us what we were near: "*You are now entering Germany, an enemy country. Be on the alert!*"'

They met their guide from the company they were relieving. He told MacDonald to remove his silver captain's bars as they might attract a sniper. They moved on. 'We crossed a slight knoll and the anti-tank wall of the Siegfried Line came suddenly into view. It looked like a prehistoric monster coiled around the hillsides, the concrete dragon's teeth were like scales upon the monster's back – or maybe headstones in a kind of crazy cemetery.'

Finally they reached their position, a small farmhouse. They went down into the cellar. It was crowded with unshaven soldiers 'in every conceivable sleeping position on the floor'. They were commanded by a 1st Lieutenant whose 'eyes were bloodshot and a half-week's beard covered his face. His voice trembled and he would start at the slightest noise.' The new boys were in the line.

Some of the troops didn't even have a farmhouse roof over their heads. They lived, ate, fought, slept – and sometimes died – in a hole. A BBC correspondent, visiting the line that week, talked to an angry GI who asked him if he had ever slept in a hole. Before the BBC man had a chance to reply the GI snorted, 'Of course, you haven't! You've never slept in a hole in the ground which you've dug while somebody tries to kill you, a hole dug as quick as you can. It's an open grave, but graves don't fill with water.' As the reporter commented, 'At night the infantryman gets some boards or a sheet of tin or an old door and puts it over one end of his slit trench, then he shovels on top of it as much dirt as he can scrape up nearby. He sleeps with his head under this. Did I say "sleeps"? Let's say "*collapses*".' As the correspondent pointed out, 'The next time you are near some muddy ditch after the rain, look at it. That's where your man lives.'

But their spell in the line wasn't as bad as that for most of the riflemen. They had come to terms with their grim environment. They had weatherproofed their foxholes, covering them with thick logs and earth. They shared this pit with a buddy. Fifty minutes each day they took off their boots and massaged each other's smelly feet to ward off trenchfoot. They stuffed old copies of the *Stars and Stripes* in between the inner and outer clothing in the fashion of the Depression hoboes in order to keep warm. They looted the abandoned houses of the area for the old-fashioned wood-and-coal burning stoves and heated their foxholes with them. There was plenty of free wood available in the forest of the Eifel-Ardennes.

They organized their day, too, as best they could. Standto was early, because the Germans were supposed to attack at first light. Whether they did or not, it was always a good time for their officers and NCOs to check if their weapons were correctly sited and that no one had 'bugged out' during the night. Breakfast would follow. The usual K-rations and canteens of 'java'. If they were lucky the cooks would whip up a batch of flapjacks. Now the GIs could relax and chat for a while – 'shoot the breeze' – though as one of them recalled afterwards, 'The language sure wouldn't have passed in anybody's drawing room,' especially as the main subject of conversation 'was the one thing they weren't getting.'

Thereafter the men would be detailed for the tasks of the day. Some would go out on the various patrols. But mostly they were mundane jobs, harmless if back-breaking: stringing new wire, filling sandbags, strengthening their foxholes.

Captain Robert Merriam of the Army's Historical Division rode along the quiet front in the Ardennes that September not far from the frontier town of Wiltz. Halfway through his journey he asked his driver where the Germans were. With a flourish, the GI said, 'See that ridge line over there just across the valley?'

Merriam nodded.

'That's it.'

'What?' Merriam enquired, who thought that they were riding just opposite the West Wall, supposedly 'bristling with guns behind every bush'.

The driver told him that was the German line and added, 'Have to be careful at night. Krauts like to sneak over patrols, just to make a social call. Ambushed a jeep in daylight the other day and got a new battalion commander. He didn't even have a chance to report in. But the only shelling we get is when a Jerry goes to the latrine. Seems they have a machine gun and a mortar there and each one fires a burst. Hope they don't get diarrhoea!'

Indeed it had become a queer kind of existence for most of these young men now stalled on this distant frontier. Staff Sergeant Henry Giles, an engineer serving with the 4th Armored Division, wrote in his diary that last week of September, 'Some of the wildest things can happen. A work detail had to go out and repair a culvert. They didn't know the password or had forgotten or something went snafu. Anyway some kid got excited, thought they were Krauts and started shooting off his rifle. Today we heard that practically the entire artillery of the 4th Armored was alerted. . . . And there's a weird story about one of the artillery gun crews. Seems they have their own private dame. One of our boys swears it's true. Says she visits them every two or three days and they queue up. Asked him why he didn't join the line. He said, much astonished, "Hell, them artillery boys'd murder you." He's a sort of mild fellow, quiet type, doesn't talk much and just the way he said it sent us into convulsions.'

A lot of the time was spent in boredom; day after day nothing happened. They indulged themselves in griping – about the officers, the chow, the mail, about the 'canteen commandos' in the rear who had beds to sleep in, clean uniforms, fresh food and, above all, *girls*. 'One man in the line,' they sneered, and *five* guys to bring up the coca-cola!'

Indeed the Com Z, the supply system, had grown mightily in the rear, spawning a huge organization which greatly outnumbered the men at the sharp end. It was not surprising that the men at the front not only envied the Com Z 'canteen commandos' but actually hated them. They knew that the Com Z men were into the rackets, depriving those at the front of their simple pleasures. As Sergeant Giles wrote in his diary, 'Wish to hell I had a smoke. Haven't even got the makings. Don't understand to save my life why we're so short.'

Soon he found out as the scandal erupted in Paris. As September gave way to October a tremendous black market in gas and cigarettes was discovered by the Army's own investigators. Eisenhower hit the roof when he heard about it. 'That some men should give way to the extraordinary temptations of the fabulous prices offered for food and cigarettes was to be expected,' he wrote after the war. 'But in this case it appeared that practically an entire unit had organized itself into an efficient gang of racketeers and was selling their articles in truck and car–load lots. Even so the blackness of the crime consisted more in the robbery of the front lines than it did in the value of the goods. I was thoroughly angry.'

The men at the sharp end were even angrier when the story broke in the *Stars and Stripes*. As Giles noted in his diary, 'It's black Friday all right. For a long time we have been hearing about a big black market gang operating in and around Paris. Today it was in the *S & S*. They say it's mostly AWOLs and that there are about 17,000 of them running loose, hijacking and stealing stuff to sell to the French. Everything from cigarettes to gas to food, tires, jeeps, all the stuff we need so bad. But there are some SOS* people in it too. And that burns the hell out of us. As if they didn't have the softest jobs of anybody, sitting on their fat asses in their plush headquarters in Paris, they have to go stealing from their own troops. There is one railway battalion involved. One damn major has sent home over thirty thousand dollars. It's the dirtiest low-down thing I ever heard of. They're up for court-martial and I hope to hell they all get life at hard labor. They *ought* to be shot.'

Eisenhower was well aware that the men at the front hated such things. They were, after all, risking their lives daily. As he wrote later: 'Morale of the combat troops had always to be carefully watched. The capacity of soldiers for absorbing punishment and enduring privations is almost inexhaustible so long as they believe they are getting a square deal.' He encouraged his subordinate commanders to set up clubs and coffee-and-doughnut wagons to provide, as he put it, 'an occasional hour of homelike atmosphere for the fighting men as far as was possible in an area thousands of miles from America.'

But that was not what the men in the line wanted. The men at the sharp end knew their lives were usually short and brutish. Coffee and doughnuts were not enough. Neither was the 'Old Groaner', or Marlene Dietrich and her million-dollar legs. What the men in the line wanted was *women*. As Patton expressed it in his characteristic fashion, 'A man who won't fuck won't fight.'

Now, as the war settled into an autumn stalemate, leave-men started to trickle back from opposite the Wall to enjoy a forty-eight or seventy-two hours of hectic activity in the big cities to the rear, Liège, Brussels, Maastricht and, above all, Paris. Pockets full of backpay – they hadn't had much use for money over the last three months – haversacks heavy with goods to sell on the black market, drunk already or soon to be in that happy state, they descended upon 'Pig Alley' (Place Pigalle), looking for one thing and one thing only.

It wasn't hard to find. Paris was packed with whores, amateur and professional. Dressed in skimpy frocks, rabbitskin 'fur' coats draped around their skinny shoulders against the autumnal cold, bare legs, usually coloured brown with make-up (silk stockings cost a fortune on the black market), feet shod in cork-soled high-heel shoes, the women loitered in doorways offering their bodies for sale to any likely looking

* Service of Supply.

71

GI. They weren't short of customers and their customers weren't particularly choosy. After all they might be dead at the end of the week.

VD rates shot upwards. Some men took precautions. They went to the Green Cross stations after intercourse for post-coital treatment. There drunken GIs stood at troughs, inserting tubes into their penis filled with anti-VD solutions and doctoring themselves with all sorts of yellow and white preventative ointments. But most of them couldn't be bothered. Why should they?

They weren't particularly pleasant young men, these men on leave from the front. They got drunk, they whored, they fought, they got sick. Their tempers were short and they were quick to take offence. The white-helmeted military policemen gave them short shrift. Troublemakers were clubbed over the head and dragged off to the nearest lock-up. But not for long. Riflemen were in short supply. The line needed them urgently.

★   ★   ★

Back in Paris Hemingway invited four of the 4th Division's battalion commanders to visit him and his new mistress, Mary Walsh, at the Hotel Ritz in Paris. At first they were well behaved. One of them asked if he could pose with Marlene Dietrich who was staying at the same hotel. She agreed and he 'arranged himself warily as stiff as at attention beside her.' But by the time they all went to eat with Congresswoman Clare Boothe Luce, wife of the owner of *Time-Life* and Mary Walsh's employer, their 'eyes were becoming a bit glazed and speech a bit slurred'. During the meal the powerful Congress member said to one drunken officer that she had been impressed by the work of the US Army Air Corps and suggested that in Belgium and Germany the infantry had surely to be of some use.

'You're darned right, babe,' the young officer replied.

'The infantry – they pinpoint an advance, don't they?' asked Mrs Luce.

'*Pinpoint it? Sweet Jesus,*' the drunken young officer exploded. 'You ought to read a book, you dumb broad. What are you doing here anyhow?' He didn't listen to her answer.

That night Mary Walsh took Hemingway to task about his guests. 'Your friends are drunks and slobs,' she snorted angrily. 'They threw up all over my bathroom. They probably lost me my job. They drove Marlene away. They may be heroes in Germany, but they stink, stink, stink here!'

Hemingway punched her.

9

DEFEAT AT METZ

General Patton had been attacking the outer fortifications of Metz for two weeks now and appeared to be getting nowhere. As always he maintained that the reason for his lack of progress was that the main bulk of the Allied Land Forces' supplies were going to Montgomery in the north. In fact the great forts surrounding Metz, some of which dated back to the 18th century, were just too tough to be cracked.

In the last week of September the XIX Tactical Air Force, supporting the Third Army, flew a series of missions against the forts, trying to do the job which the infantry had failed to do. Time and again the Thunderbolts, carrying 1,000 lb bombs and the dreaded new weapon which so far had only been used once in the campaign, napalm, fell out of the skies to drop their deadly cargo on the forts below.

Watching one such aerial attack on Fort de Verdun an observer noted, 'A pilot diving straight down for one of the turrets of the fort as a thunderous roar of enemy ack–ack rolled across the valley. The pilot came down so low that it looked as though he would crash. The plane made a quick upturn and the bombs could be plainly seen as they dropped. In a second or two a huge flame shot up. "That's napalm," one of the officers watching said, "and plenty hot for any German there."

'The ack–ack roar continued and the spectators held their breath hoping the pilot would get through. He turned and then headed down for the ack–ack with his machine guns. The pilot pulled up and out of his way to safety and a silent cheer went up from those on the observation post.'

On 27 September Colonel Yuill's 11th Infantry Regiment of the Fifth Division was ordered to attack the Metz fortifications once again. A week previously Yuill had lost virtually a whole battalion in a similar attack. But he was confident he would be able to do it this time, especially as the weather was good and he had air support.

The main objective of the assault was to be perhaps the most powerful of all the thirty-nine forts guarding Metz. It was Fort Driant, named after a French hero of the Battle of Verdun in 1916, Colonel Driant, who had held out against all that the Kaiser's army had been able to throw at him. It was located five miles to the south-west of the city on the western bank of the Moselle, and, like all the other forts around Metz, it was covered by the guns of its neighbours, so that any attacker would not just face the guns of a single fort but those of three or four others.

Fort Driant's defences were built around four steel casemates and a central fort. What the ill-prepared Americans didn't know (for at this time they had no plans of the Metz forts) was that there was, in addition, an intricate and interlinked system of pillboxes, shelters and minefields, and that each casemate was connected to the central fort by an underground tunnel. Men could be moved from one defensive position to another in an emergency, protected by six-foot-thick ferro-concrete. Fort Driant was going to be a very tough nut to crack.

At eight thirty on the morning of Wednesday, 27 September, US fighter bombers from their field at Etain, which was now Patton's HQ, took off to begin the preliminary softening up of what was probably the strongest fortified place in the whole of Europe.

Again and again they fell out of the sky while the spectators watched with bated breath, cheered by the black mushrooms of smoke rising into the sky, telling themselves that no one could survive a bombardment like that, even the defenders of Fort Driant.

The planes departed and for a little while there was silence. But not for long. Suddenly the artillery of General Irwin's Fifth Division cracked into action. Before he had become an infantry divisional commander, Irwin had been an artilleryman. He knew the value of artillery to soften up an objective before the infantry attacked. Relentlessly, although shells were rationed – as usual Patton was trying to do too much, attacking not only at Metz but also in the Saar Valley – his guns laid down a tremendous barrage on Fort Driant. The walls of the great fort disappeared in the fog of war.

H-hour was at two o'clock. The men of Yuill's companies rose from their foxholes and started to advance. They cheered themselves up with the thought that nobody could have survived that tremendous bombardment from air and land.

For a while nothing happened. They had achieved surprise. The

Germans had not expected the *Amis* to attack. Perhaps they had thought that the softening-up preparations would go on much longer. But now the defenders could see the long slow lines of attackers through their slits. '*Die Amis kommen!*' they yelled.

The attackers quickened their pace. Up front the men of 'F' Company prepared their Bangalore torpedoes, a British invention stretching back to the 19th century, a long pole with an explosive charge at the end. This would be thrust under the barbed wire of the outer defences, in some places twenty feet thick, to destroy the barbed wire. But already the hidden German machine gunners were scything the wire from left to right with a withering fire.

But the infantry, feeling naked and defenceless in the open now that their own guns had ceased firing, pressed on. Desperately their officers and NCOs urged them to quicken their pace. But they were growing ever more reluctant to face that lethal fire.

A squad of 'F' Company, exploding their Bangalore torpedoes in front of the wire, managed to blast their way through foot after foot of barbed wire. But hardly had they done so than they were spotted by a German machine gunner in one of the hidden pillboxes. He spun his Spandau round and started firing at them. They flopped to the ground, trying to bury themselves into the wet cold earth, as the tracer zipped over their heads. There was nothing else they could do.

Everywhere the attackers started to go to ground and dig in, wielding their shovels furiously. They knew what was going to happen now. They had lost the element of surprise. Soon the Germans would retaliate.

Five minutes later, as their machine guns swept the whole front with a hail of fire, their mortars crashed into action and bombs began to rain out of the sky. Neighbouring forts joined in and now the infantry of the 11th Infantry Regiment could do nothing but cower at the bottom of their holes as the ground trembled all around them.

Finally the infantry began to withdraw in little groups, praying that they wouldn't stumble into a minefield in the darkness. As the skies opened up and rain started to pour down, the weary angry infantrymen started to dig fresh holes for the night. All the day's efforts had been in vain. They were back where they had started. They hadn't gained a single inch of ground. Fort Driant and Metz had beaten Patton yet again.

★   ★   ★

On the following morning Colonel Yuill, General Irwin and General Walker, commander of Patton's XX Corps, drove to Etain to talk to the

Army Commander about Fort Driant. Although the previous day's aerial and artillery bombardment had failed to dent the Fort and had indeed raised the morale of the defenders, and although the 11th Infantry had got no further than three hundred yards from Fort Driant's moat, Walker and Yuill were eager for another attack. Yuill's enthusiasm was shared by the Corps Commander. The latter suggested that the reason for the failure of the previous day's assault was the lack of aggressive leadership.

'Red' Irwin, the commander of the Fifth Division, was not so sure. He irritated the man who had given him his divisional command by pointing out that they knew virtually nothing about Fort Driant's defences. Irwin said that the Fort was more intricate and powerful than they had anticipated. Besides his men weren't trained in tackling fortresses; they needed special training for an operation like that.

But both Walker and Patton were for continuing the attack. Irwin was on the spot. In the US Army it didn't go down well if you criticized your Corps Commander. You could well lose your own command if you did so and Irwin, who had been serving since 1915, knew that at his age he'd never get another chance if he were dismissed now. He stared at Patton and spoke his piece, knowing that he was risking his career by doing so. Nevertheless he said, 'My men need rest, sir, and special training in this kind of operation. I think the fort ought to be taken by encirclement, but we have no troops for that either.'

Patton breathed out and Irwin waited for the explosion to come. But it didn't. For now two of Patton's own staff joined in to support Irwin. General Gay, Deputy Chief-of-Staff, and his assistant, Colonel Maddox, who had made an extensive reconnaissance before Yuill's attack and had then watched the attack the following day, didn't believe that there had been any lack of good leadership. They also felt that the morale of the men was good. It was the plan that was wrong. Gay and Maddox told Patton it was madness to assault Fort Driant and Metz frontally; the enemy's defences were simply too strong. In their opinion what was needed was what Irwin had suggested, a double envelopment of Metz with three infantry and two armoured divisions. Anything less, they warned, would not be sufficient to take Fort Driant.

Patton was not convinced, nor was Walker. His pride had been hurt because he had twice failed to capture Driant. Patton was no different. His Third Army had not lost a battle yet. He was not going to lose this one, cost what it may.

Again Irwin asked for time. His Fifth Division had suffered 3,000 battle casualties during September and something like the same number of non-battle ones. At this moment, he told Patton, the Fifth was absorbing 4,000 replacements, just over a quarter of its official strength and most of these replacements were straight from the States, with, in some cases, only eighteen weeks of infantry training behind them.

Patton was adamant. On the next day Eisenhower was coming to Etain. If he approved the plan, then the attack would go in as planned. On 29 September Eisenhower came to the modest château, just outside Etain's main square, which housed Patton's HQ. After lunch Patton's plan for the reduction of Fort Driant was put to him. Although four days earlier Eisenhower had ordered Patton to go on the defensive for the time being, he didn't object to the attack. It was presented to him as a local manoeuvre, an assault on a fort which could be taken by a single battalion. In his own memoir, *War As I Knew It*, Patton falsified the real situation when he wrote: 'The Fifth Division believed that Driant . . . could be taken with a battalion.'

General Irwin didn't believe any such thing. He was the prime advocate of the five-division encirclement assault. But Eisenhower knew nothing of that nor of the real strength of Fort Driant, manned by 900 fanatical Germans. And, as was usual with the Supreme Commander, he didn't go up front to have a look. The Supreme Commander's rare sorties to the front normally never went any closer than a divisional headquarters. So Eisenhower agreed to Patton's plan.

And that was the end to any objections to the plan of attack. That day Fifth Division was ordered to prepare to attack not only Fort Driant but also 'Verdun', the fortified group west of the Moselle. The assault would begin on Tuesday, 3 October. Patton had got his way once again.

But there was a sting in the tail. Later that day Patton was told he was about to lose his 7th Armored Division. They were to join General Hodges' 1st Army up north. He was also ordered to assign two divisions, including the 83rd Infantry Division, one of Patton's favourites, to fight their way to the Luxemburg border and link up with Hodges' 1st Army there. These two divisions, however, would still be under Patton's control. But the worst news was that he was to give up XV Corps to General Patch's US 7th Army coming up from the south. Thus he would lose his veteran 79th Infantry Division, plus that other veteran division, which had been fighting since 1941, Leclerc's 2nd French Armored Division.

That day it must have seemed to Patton that Eisenhower was deliberately wrecking his beloved Third Army. His dream of breaking through the West Wall in ten days was shattered. He expressed his disappointment to his friend and senior staff officer, General Gay, 'Well, Hap; how would you like to go to China and serve under Admiral Nimitz?'

There was only one consolation, though it wasn't much. At that moment his XV Corps on the Third Army's right flank was under severe attack by the Germans. There was no way they could disengage and join Patch's Seventh.

★   ★   ★

Both XV Corps' 79th and 4th Armored Divisions were under attack by von Manteuffel's Fifth Army. In the case of General Wood's 4th Armored, he was being attacked by elements of two panzer brigades, a panzer division and a panzer grenadier division. Fortunately the Americans were located on high ground from which they dominated the battlefield. All the same the pressure was very great.

With their ranks filled with replacements, some of whom had never even *seen* a tank (Nat Fraenkel recalled a 'gunner' who wore glasses and pleaded with him, 'Just don't let me fire at any of our own boys!'), the Fourth fought back as best they could in the terrible weather.

One day before Eisenhower made the decision to allow Patton to continue his attack on Fort Driant, a small wiry Texan from Fort Worth, 1st Lieutenant James Fields, took the men of his 'A' Company of the 10th Armored Infantry Battalion to the top of Hill 265. They had been sent up to fill a gap left by two platoons that had been cut to pieces by the German attack. Fifty-five men had gone up the hill the day before. After fourteen hours only thirteen had returned. It was indicative of the severity of the fighting.

Now, under the cover of darkness, Fields ordered his men to dig in. They spent a relatively quiet night. But at dawn whistles suddenly shrilled. There were harsh commands in German. Then they were there, coming out of the gloom carrying machine pistols.

'Krauts,' someone yelled. 'Here they come!'

Firing broke out immediately. The infantrymen in their pits poured on the fire but the Germans kept advancing. But their pace was slower and there were great gaps in their ranks. The firing intensified. Just as suddenly as they had attacked, the Germans broke and started streaming back to the rear.

Then Fields heard one of his men scream, 'I'm hit! Medic!' But the squad had no medics with it. Fields dashed in the direction of the call for help as one of his squad leaders screamed with agony as a slug slammed into his head. Fields swung round, Colt in his fist. A German was standing only yards away. He raised the pistol, but the German beat him to the draw. The slug struck him in the face and ripped through his left cheek. It went through his face and out of his right cheek, taking most of his teeth with it. Feeling giddy and nauseated, he would dearly have liked to lie down. His mouth was filled with blood and the fragments of his jaw. But he knew there was no time for that. He had to keep control of his little band of hard-pressed soldiers. He ripped the gory mess out of his mouth, realizing that he could no longer speak. Still he refused to be evacuated. The Germans attacked again and he gave his orders by hand signals and pencilled messages passed from foxhole to foxhole.

His wounds started to bleed heavily. He was spitting blood. Still he refused to give up. He thrust a wound pack into his mouth and, holding another compress against his holed right cheek, he fired with his left hand. Somehow he kept his command together under intense enemy pressure.

Three Panther tanks rumbled up and the German gunners started to shoot up the line of foxholes. Fields rose from his foxhole and, firing left-handed, shot the commander of one of the tanks dead. Now his squad poured their concentrated fire on the other two German tanks. They fled.

'I'll never know why they didn't overrun us,' Fields said later. 'We didn't have a thing in the world to stop them other than a bunch of fighting mad doughs who just wouldn't give up. My platoon was wonderful that day. No one ever thought of withdrawing. At one time those tanks were so damned close that they were firing direct fire at the tops of our foxholes with their 75s.'

At noon that day the Germans withdrew and Fields decided he would get some treatment for his wounds. Assigning a sergeant to take charge, he somehow covered the half mile back to the battalion aid station. But even here his sense of duty prevailed. Before he would allow himself to be taken away by ambulance to a field hospital for treatment he insisted on drawing a picture sketch of his own and the enemy positions for the battalion commander. Then he passed out.

James Fields was the first member of the Fighting Fourth to be awarded America's highest award for gallantry, the Congressional Medal of Honor.

★   ★   ★

While Patton's 83rd Division attacked north-east to seize the Luxemburg towns of Echternach and Grevenmacher to secure the link with Hodges' 1st Army, his Fifth Division, as planned, attacked Fort Driant for the third time.

This time the hard-pressed men of the 11th's 2nd Battalion were given all the support they required. First there was an aerial bombardment, followed by the whole weight of XX Corps's artillery. In addition they were supported by tanks, manned by specially picked men, plus 'tankdozers', Sherman tanks fitted with bulldozer shovels for filling in ditches and thrusting aside obstacles. Engineers went in with the infantry. They, too, had been given all the equipment they had asked for for dealing with fortifications − flame-throwers, Bangalore torpedoes, satchel and pole charges, plus 'snakes'. These were long pipes filled with high explosive which were to be pushed into the thick barbed wire screens and exploded, thus destroying the wire and leaving the way free for the infantry.

But although the infantry had more success than they had had the previous two occasions, they were still unable to penetrate the fort itself. One company alone suffered fifty per cent casualties before it gave up. Another company which penetrated the wire and first line of bunkers was forced to go to ground under overwhelming fire. There it remained dug in for four days, unable to move either forward or back.

Here and there individual soldiers penetrated the fortifications. In scenes reminiscent of 1916 when Colonel Driant had held his fort at Verdun against the attacks of up to 10,000 German soldiers, these soldiers crawled down shafts, threw grenades into darkened passages, tried to knock our ventilation systems and flushed out the tunnels with their flame throwers. A Private Holmlund recalled climbing on to the roof of one of the occupied bunkers, kicking off the covers of the ventilation shafts and stuffing Bangalore torpedoes down them. 'I could hear 'em swearing and trampling over one another trying to get out.' Holmlund won a medal for his bravery that day but was killed a little later.

For the Germans had the great advantage of being able to move from one part of the fortifications to the other in their underground tunnels whenever danger threatened, while the American attackers were always in full view of the defenders behind their thick concrete walls and the gunners of the other forts supporting Driant. Losses were high in the first three assault companies, almost sixty per cent in some cases. Still Colonel Yuill persisted with his attack, supported by Patton who snarled, 'If it takes every man in the XX Corps, I cannot allow an attack by this army to fail.'

But it was failing, whether Patton liked it or not. On the same day that the Commanding General made that statement the officer in charge of Yuill's 'G' Company signalled HQ: 'The situation is critical. Another couple more barrages and another counter-attack and we're sunk. We have no men, our equipment is shot and just can't go. The troops of 'G' are done. They're just there – what's left of them. Enemy has infiltrated and pinned down what is here. We cannot advance, nor can 'K' Co. 'B' Co is in the same shape. We may be able to hold till dark but if anything happens this afternoon I can make no predictions. The enemy artillery is butchering these troops and we have nothing left to hold with. We cannot get out to get our wounded and there are a hell of a lot of dead and missing. There is only one answer to the way things stand. First either to withdraw and saturate it with heavy bombers or reinforce with a hell of a strong force. . . . This is just a suggestion, but if we want this damned fort let's get the stuff required to take it and then go. Right now you haven't got it. Gerrie, Capt. Inf.'

That odd disjointed message was indicative of the state of mind of the attackers. For the third time the Fifth Infantry Division had been given an impossible mission. The opposition was too great.

In the end even General Bradley, who relied upon Patton's support to sabotage what he believed was Montgomery's influence on the Supreme Commander, lost his patience. As he wrote after the war, 'During October Patton undertook an unauthorized pecking campaign against the enemy fortress position at Metz. When I found him probing those battlements I appealed impatiently to him, "For God's sake, George, lay off. I promise you you'll get your chance. When we get going again you can far more easily pinch Metz and take it from behind. Why bloody your nose in this pecking campaign?"'

It was exactly the same plan that General Irwin had had right from the start.

Patton nodded as if he agreed, but still the costly diversion continued. He told Bradley 'We're using Metz to blood the new divisions.' Bradley knew that that statement was patently absurd. There were no new divisions in the Metz area. The only new troops being blooded were the poorly trained replacements straight from the States who were totally unprepared for the fight against the forts. All the same Bradley did nothing to stop his subordinate from wasting their lives in futile attacks against steel and concrete.

Now, with Hodges' First Army stalled at Aachen (the city wouldn't fall till the last week of October) and Patton's in a similar position at Metz, the battle would continue till the first week of December. There remained only one US army that still might have a chance of reaching the Rhine before Hitler's counter-attack began. It was General Patch's Seventh Army coming up from the south into the Alsatian Vosges Mountains, the last natural barrier before the Rhenish plain beyond. Now it was the turn of 'America's Forgotten Army'.*

* The official history of the US Seventh Army, which is still serving in Germany, didn't appear until 1993, fifty years after it was formed.

9. A soldier of the Waffen SS during the defence of Metz.

10. Army bivouac in the woods above Metz.

11. It was here on the River Our that the first US troops crossed into Germany at 6pm on 11 September, 1944. Luxembourg is on the right, Germany on the left.

12. Another gateway to the Third Reich.

13. Troops of the US 7th Army in Saarguemines plan the advance to
    Saarbrüken..

14. 7th Army reaches the Rhine at last.

15. The author, in 1995, looks at dragons' teeth that were once part of the Westwall near Hosingen to the west of Wiltz.

16. Battlefield debris found by the author along the Westwall in 1995.

II

OCTOBER–NOVEMBER, 1944

'Win the war by forty-four'
'Stay alive in forty-five'

Two unofficial slogans of Seventh Army GIs, December 1943 and December, 1944.

1

INTO THE VOSGES

It was Friday, 9 July, 1943. For most of the voyage from North Africa to Sicily the invasion convoy, the greatest fleet ever assembled, had had calm weather. But during the dog watch a wind had sprung up. It freshened almost immediately and by the minute grew in intensity. A hot wind straight from the heart of the Sahara struck the huge convoy. Within minutes the ships, packed with troops, were ploughing up and down the grey-green sea as if on a giant roller coaster. The skippers of the troop transports strained to keep to the all-important timetables.

On board the *Monrovia*, his command ship, Patton, who would land with his men at the Sicilian coastal town of Gela, asked the met. officer to come to his cabin. 'How long will this storm last?' Patton demanded.

'It will calm down by D-day, sir,' the weatherman replied.

General Patton gave him a wintry look and said threateningly, 'It had better.' The weatherman fled.

By midnight, just as the *Monrovia*'s radar picked up the Sicilian coast, the storm began to abate. By midnight it had died away and Patton knew some relief. The invasion could go ahead after all. It was his witching hour.

At midnight his staff assembled on the bridgedeck as the commanding general of the first US army to invade Europe in the Second World War made his appearance. Patton, spick and span as always, made a little speech. 'Gentlemen', he said, 'it's now one minute past midnight 9/10

85

July, 1943, and I have the honor and privilege to activate the Seventh United States Army. This is the first army in history to be activated after midnight and baptized in blood before daylight.'

Admiral Hewitt, the task force naval commander, signalled to his aide. The latter opened the door. In marched an honour guard carrying a gift from the US Navy for Patton – a brand new flag for a brand new army. Patton started to cry. But as one of the naval men present, Commander Brittain, recorded later, 'But I could see the fire of pride in his eyes. It was to him not a ship's deck he stood, but a peak of glory.'

Patton lasted as the effective commander of the new Seventh Army for thirty days, the length of the Sicilian campaign. The famous slapping incident cost him his command. His divisions were taken away from him and sent to Italy to join his hated rival, General Clark's Fifth Army. 'Clark was trying to be nice, but it makes my flesh creep to be with him.' For his part Patton remained behind, miserable and lonely, commanding some 5,000 men.

Even the official US history of the campaign refers to his dash for Palermo as 'almost a publicity agent's stunt'. But he *had* put his Seventh Army firmly on the map. Patton's flamboyant style, his celebrated quips, his profanity, ensured that he was good copy for the correspondents and ensured that he and his Seventh were always in the headlines.

Patton's relief by Eisenhower was followed in due course by the appointment of two commanders who would direct the fortunes of the Seventh for the rest of the war and put their stamp on it, once the Seventh was reactivated for the invasion of Southern France in August, 1944.

The first to arrive was General Jacob Devers, a 57-year-old artilleryman, who in his twenties had played polo with Patton, but he had nothing of the latter's flair and personality. He would become Eisenhower's deputy in the Middle East and in due course would command the Sixth Army Group, to which the Seventh and the First French Army then belonged. But, despite his great responsibilities, Devers would remain unknown to the general public. Of all America's major wartime commanders he was the only one who would never have his biography written.

Eisenhower didn't like him. Indeed, when asked by the US Department of War to list the abilities of his various subordinate generals, Eisenhower ranked the Army Group Commander at twenty-fourth, lower than several humble corps commanders. Worse, he was the only general of the twenty-eight involved on whom Eisenhower had something negative to report, writing that Devers was 'often inaccurate in statements and evaluations. . . . He has not so far produced among the seniors of the American organization here a feeling of trust and confidence.'

Eisenhower ensured that Devers never received much publicity and, as Devers himself was a character lacking in colour, his Seventh Army was never much publicized.

Another problem was that Devers' Sixth was relegated to a side-show – first the invasion of Southern France, then the long slog to Alsace and, finally, after being the last Allied Army to cross the Rhine, the drive into Southern Germany. While Patton's Third made the headlines, Devers' Seventh did the foot-slogging.

The situation was not helped when the new commander of the new Seventh Army was appointed in March, 1944. General Alexander Patch, a tall man with thinning red hair which had gained him the nickname of 'Sandy' at West Point, had, unlike his army group commander, a fine combat record. In the First World War he had fought with the 'Big Red One' in France in 1917. Thereafter he had trained raw recruits for the infantry, gaining for himself the reputation of being a tough disciplinarian. In 1942 he was given the task of whipping the Americal (American-Caledonian) Division into shape. That done, he was ordered to take his pick-up division and relieve the hard-pressed Marines on Guadalcanal. It was his first battle command, but within two months he had ended the campaign there successfully.

Now he would lead the Seventh for the rest of the war. But, like Devers, Patch wasn't good copy. He never succeeded in getting the publicity for his divisions which they richly deserved.

★   ★   ★

One month after the invasion of Southern France Patch's Seventh Army had reached the foot of the Vosges. Behind them they left a string of famous French cities which they had liberated with hardly a fight. For the German 19th Army, commanded by General Frederick Wiese, did not want a stand-up battle. Time and again Wiese had avoided the traps set for him by Patch, sacrificing his rear guard of Russians, Georgians and the like to the Americans so that he could extricate his important German formations. His intention was to get the bulk of these to the Franco-German frontier where they could be used in the defence of the Reich. No wonder the troops called it the 'champagne campaign'.

Casualties were light, the weather splendid, the wine flowed, the natives
were friendly and the girls were eager.

In the third week of September the Seventh and the French First Army
turned eastwards. The German border was only 100 miles away and
Wiese was still in retreat. Before them lay the Moselle, the Vosges, in
particular the High Vosges, a north-east/south-west range which formed
a major obstacle to the Plain of Alsace and the River Rhine. That week
the G2 of Patch's VI Corps, commanded by General Truscott, one of
the few US generals ever to have stood up to Patton, warned, 'The
Vosges Mountains will make an excellent position from which to defend
and it is doubtful that the enemy will evacuate it without being forced
to do so. 'The G2's warning was apt. The days of the champagne
campaign were nearly over.

Still, Truscott ordered the Moselle to be forced. His 36th Texas
Division would lead off the attack, followed by the 45th and 3rd
Divisions. All were veterans of the fighting in Italy and now in France.

The men of the Texas Division were not happy with their assign-
ment. Most of them still bore memories of their terrible crossing of the
River Rapido in Italy, where, through lack of preparation, they had
suffered 3,000 casualties.* The veterans of that bloody fiasco noted the
similarity between the deadly S-bend of the Italian river which had
been their undoing and the curve of the Moselle. That was not their
only problem. There were no roads leading through the forest to the
river, only trails. How were they to bring up the heavy weapons and
supplies?

But for once the men of the 36th Division were lucky, for a while.
Guides were asked for and, of all people, the 70-year-old mayor of the
village of Raon-aux-Bois, a former naval officer, offered his services. The
staff officers were doubtful. After all the Frenchman was pretty old for a
night jaunt up the rugged trail through the forest. But when Mayor
Gribelin told the officers what he knew, 'they almost kissed him,' as one
GI explained to the reporter from 'Yank' magazine.

It appeared that Gribelin knew a jeep-sized path through the woods
which led to a shallow ford in the Moselle where the water was only
waist-deep. But some of the staff officers were still hesitant. The Vosges
marked the linguistic border between French and German-speakers and

---

* At the time the surviving officers swore a secret oath that they would bring General Clark to trial after
the war for the mess he had made of the Rapido Crossing. They managed to do so, but the charge was
not proven.

Alsace to the east of the range had been incorporated into the Third Reich in 1940. But General Truscott was breathing down the neck of the staff. So they took a chance. As the Mayor explained that he used the ford as a short cut to visit his daughter who lived in German-held territory, which seemed genuine enough, the staff officers decided to use him as their guide. So they set off at midnight through rain and fog, three battalions of the Texas Division's 141st Infantry Regiment led by the old man.

By one o'clock that morning General Dahlquist, commanding the 36th Division, had three battalions strung out on a three-mile stretch of the river. Now the veterans of the Rapido eyed the steep, heavily wooded opposite side. Were the enemy waiting for them over there just as they had been at the Rapido?

The old Frenchman pointed to his ford. But since the last time he had been this way the river had flooded. It was now shoulder-deep. Undaunted, an engineer, Corporal Walter Lindsey, volunteered to get a rope across. Taking off his boots and helmet and tying the rope to his belt, he swam across the river and the rest of the 1st Battalion followed, fighting the stiff current and holding their weapons above their heads.

As the lead elements reached the other side the enemy spotted them. A red flare sailed into the air. Suddenly German mortars and machine guns opened up. Mortar bombs started to drop into the water, throwing up violent spouts of water. The lifeline was shot in two but another was rigged up at a more sheltered spot. But it would be afternoon before all the 1st Battalion was across the river.

At nearby Eloyes the 141st's 2nd Battalion made a co-ordinated assault. The Germans reacted violently. But the men of the 2nd persisted. All the same resistance was so strong that it would be a few days before the 36th Division could throw a bridge across the Moselle. But, thanks to the mayor, this had been no second Rapido.

* * *

At Epinal, the 45th Division was also forcing the Moselle. Again resistance was stiff. One company managed to get across, but met such withering fire that it was forced to retreat across the river, leaving one fifth of its number dead and dying. But unlike their partners, the 36th, they were a lucky division. They slogged it out with the Germans in their first serious fight since they had landed in France, and they made it.

It was the same for O'Daniel's Third Infantry Division, only tougher. The 'Rock of the Marne' men were fighting through well-wooded, mountainous terrain, made more difficult by the ankle-deep mud after the persistent rains of the last few days. Slowly they edged their way to the Moselle, fighting German roadblocks and snipers every few hundred yards.

The 3rd Battalion of the Division's 30th Infantry was stopped dead for a while that day by snipers and crossfire. With fire coming from three sides, the infantry were unable to advance. That day the Division's 7th Infantry reported, 'The fighting in the woods is pretty tough. The undergrowth makes movement difficult. The Battalion has been having quite a fire fight.'

It was no different in the Division's third regiment, the 15th. Staff Sergeant Audie Murphy was 19 but looked all of fourteen and had already killed more men than many a professional soldier; he was ordered to go back and pick up some green replacements to make up the new gaps in the line. As he collected them together, the air above him was rent by the howl of a mortar bomb. It exploded nearby in a ball of red flame. Murphy yelled with pain and blacked out. Later he recorded, 'When I come to I am sitting beside a crater with a broken carbine in my hands. My head aches, my eyes burn and I cannot hear. The acrid greasy taste of burnt powder fills my mouth.'

But he had not lost the proverbial luck of the Irish. He was, after all, the last man left of his Company which had started out for Sicily the year before. All the rest were dead or in hospital. If the bomb had landed a few feet closer he would have been as dead as the two replacements. They lay only feet away.

General Patch threw in his new corps, the one taken from Patton, Wade Haislip's XV Corps. It consisted of the US 79th Infantry Division and Leclerc's 2nd French Armored, which in August had taken Paris and was now intent on capturing Strasbourg. But that wasn't to be, not yet.

The new corps was low on gas and ammunition. Nor did it possess the heavy artillery to batter its way through the forests and mountains ahead. Still Haislip was a fighter. He ordered the infantry of the 'Cross of Lorraine' division into the attack. Their first objective was to be the Forest of Parroy behind which the Germans had built a continuous line of bunkers, trenches and anti-tank ditches.

Surprisingly enough the 79th's advance to the edge of the forest went without trouble. Army Intelligence had indicated that the forest was defended by the 15th Panzer Grenadier Division, a veteran of the fighting in North Africa and Italy. But the two regiments, the 315th and

313th, taking part in the attack met no real opposition until they had penetrated the trees.

All hell broke loose as the American covering barrage ceased and the infantry were left to do their job. With a rusty creak, pine trees snapping like matchwood, several Mark IV tanks started racing from their hiding place straight down the central road, heading for the astonished Americans. The counter-attack had begun.

By nightfall all was confusion and panic in the forest. German snipers and infiltrators were everywhere. Time and again little groups of grenadiers, armed with machine pistols and stick grenades, launched attacks on the split-up squads of American infantry. There followed a few minutes of bitter action in which neither side gave or expected quarter. Then the surviving Germans would vanish again into the fog, leaving behind the dead and dying. By nightfall on the first day of the attack into the Forêt de Parroy the American assault had come to a standstill. The GIs huddled in their foxholes under constant German artillery fire. By the time they were through, they would have suffered two thousand battle casualties.

★   ★   ★

Back in August when Devers' Sixth Army Group had landed in the Riviera, General de Lattre de Tassigny, the commander of his 1st French Army, had told his officers, half in jest, 'Whatever you do, don't crush the vines.' Even a war could not be allowed to destroy the precious vines. But it had been that kind of battle. 'Booze and babes and a little bit of battle,' the GIs had quipped.

Now the bubbly had gone flat. Now the Seventh Army's progress had turned into a slow, gruelling slogging match with the weary troops plodding up and down hills, through mud which bogged down their trucks and tanks, the rain falling all the time. Back on the plain before they had entered the Vosges, many of the Seventh's GIs had bought picture postcards to send back home as souvenirs. Cheaply coloured, sentimental things, they had featured 'Big bosomed babes holding bunches of grapes between their toothpaste smiles and wearing picturesque Alsatian clothes,' as one disgruntled sergeant described them that autumn, 'or else pictures of mountain scenery with happy, healthy people and an over-ripe moon in the background.'

But that had been in the plain. In the mountains it was different. As the sergeant snorted, echoing the feelings of his comrades, 'The babes weren't beautiful any more. The people were hungry and thin. As for the scenery, that forest full of Christmas trees was lousy with snipers, those streams only made your feet wetter and the full moon shone on hills making the GIs curse, thinking of the long *fucking* climb and the *fucking* mud, and the *fucking* mud on the other side as well.'

The champagne campaign was over. The time of despair had begun.

2

THE BOY MARSHAL

They shot the first eight of Colonel Franks's 2nd SAS Regiment on 8 October. They had belonged to the rearguard party under the command of Lieutenant Dill. They had been left behind to cover Franks as he led the rest of his survivors through the Vosges to the lines of the US Seventh Army. On 8 October Franks reached the US lines and waited for Dill to join him, but Dill had been out of luck. On the afternoon of the 7th he and his rearguard had been surprised and overpowered by a German armoured unit. The tankers had immediately handed the SAS over to one of the special police-Gestapo *Jagdkommandos* (hunting commandos) now roaming the Vosges, trying to liquidate the Maquis and whoever helped them. In this case it was a hunting commando led by a Captain Ernst, based on the little town of Saales.

SS Captain Hans Ernst had already ordered another group of SAS men shot a week before in the St Dié area. Before that Ernst's hunting commando, made up of Germans, twenty French civilians and some Arabs, had shot captured members of Paddy Mayne's 1st SAS Regiment in August near his base at Angers on the Loire. Now he decided to rid himself of the burden of these remaining 'parachute terrorists', who had refused to talk even under extreme pressure. He felt fully justified in carrying out the death sentence without recourse to law or a court-martial. Hadn't the Führer himself issued an order stating that any enemy soldier found behind German lines, even if he was in uniform, was to be summarily executed? The Leader's secret *Kommandobefehl* was the only justification that Ernst needed.

In two closed trucks the eight SAS men were taken into the forest, past the rough-and-ready defence line the Germans had already dug on the forward slopes of the Vosges. When the trucks were well away from any habitation they turned off up a narrow track. For a moment the truck stopped so that *Unterscharführer* Geiger could be posted as a sentry to keep away any possible witnesses. The party drove on till a suitable spot was found for the executions.

Under the command of *Hauptsturmführer* Golkel (for Ernst was what the Germans call a *Schreibtischtäter**; he would never soil his hands with such filthy work) the prisoners were led away one by one to the edge of a narrow ditch. Here they were made to strip naked. Then they were ordered to kneel. One of the SS placed the muzzle of his pistol behind the condemned man's head and blew the back of his skull off. The naked body then fell into the ditch. When the slaughter was over the bodies were buried. They were sure that no one would ever find them in that remote place.

They were wrong. A year later when the 'secret hunters' as they called themselves, that small body of unofficial SAS (the SAS had already been disbanded), were looking for the remains of their dead comrades and their murderers, a member of the team, Sergeant Major 'Dusty' Rhodes, who had been a horticulturalist in civilian life, decided that a 'certain area of growth was slightly different from the rest of the surrounding habitat'. He and the others decided to dig. 'On my first attempt I turned up a chap's toe and I knew then that we'd found the eight missing SAS personnel.'

Rhodes put the toe into a matchbox. It would be part of the evidence that would soon help to put some of the killers on trial. But that was in the future. There would be more prisoners from the 1st and 2nd SAS Regiments murdered that October and, in the case of three of them, burnt to death.

But there were still teams parachuting into the Vosges. For the Seventh Army was fighting practically blind. The reprisals carried out by the *Jagdkommandos* and their French allies had badly scared the Maquis of the area. As a result they were keeping a low profile and little about the Germans' intentions and defences was filtering through to US Intelligence.

Thus, while Hemingway and Mary Walsh were enjoying a pleasant lunch at their 'headquarters' in the Paris Ritz, a young lieutenant came up to their table and introduced himself. He said he was Lieutenant Prince Poniatowski, scion of a famous Polish family, presently serving in the OSS, and he had some bad news. He had been sent to Paris personally by General 'Iron Mike' O'Daniel, the commander of the US Third

---

* Literally a 'writing desk killer', ie one who just signs the orders which others have to carry out.

Division, from the Vosges. 'Iron Mike', who had just lost his own 19-year-old son in combat in Holland, wanted Hemingway to know that his son, also in the OSS, had been wounded and captured while on patrol in the Vosges. After five months in Europe as a war correspondent, the real war had finally reached Hemingway.

He had been very proud of his son, 21-year-old Jack Hemingway, when he had volunteered from his safe billet with the US Military Police to join the OSS. In the summer of 1944 he had jumped into France with his OSS team and had thereafter carried out intelligence and reconnaissance work for Patch's Seventh.

Not far from where Audie Murphy had lost his two replacements that day, Jack Hemingway, a Captain Justin Green and a Frenchman had been trying to infiltrate the German lines in the forest when the Germans had surprised them with machine-gun fire and grenades. Green had been hit in the foot, the Frenchman mortally wounded and Hemingway wounded by five bullets in the shoulder and arm.

'We were lying there,' Jack Hemingway recalled after the war; 'when an Austrian lieutenant looked at my dogtags and said, "*Sprechen sie Deutsch?*" And I said, "*Non, je parle français.*" Then he spoke French. He asked, "Were you ever at Schroons?"' [Schrums, Austria]

Jack Hemingway replied, 'Yes, when I was a little boy.'

'Do you remember anyone named Kitty?' the officer of the Austrian 2nd Mountain Division asked.

'Yes, she was my nurse,' Hemingway answered.

The Austrian then informed the surprised youngster that Kitty had been his girlfriend; that he had known and admired his father, adding, 'Do not be nervous. I know who you are and I am a great admirer of your father's work.'

Jack Hemingway, who knew that his father had earlier in the war written a preface to a collection of tales called *Men at War* in which he had advocated that all SS men should be castrated, relaxed a little. A few hours later Hemingway, instead of being shot like the SAS men, was transported to Colmar to the rear and patched up before being sent to a regular POW camp in Germany where he survived the war.

But at the Ritz that Sunday Hemingway didn't know that. He was very worried. More wine was brought and he fired questions at the young 'Lieutenant Prince'. Mary Walsh could feel 'Ernest's temperature, blood pressure, anxiety, anger and frustration rising to some point of explosion with no safety valve apparent.' The wine started to talk. Hemingway began to fabricate all sorts of crazy plans to rescue his son.

'Haven't we got a plan of their hospital system there?' he demanded. His idea was to land a small plane, perhaps an artillery spotter, near the German hospital where Jack was being held and rescue him. 'If we made a surprise drop, we could get him out,' he urged. 'We ought to be able to make a heist.'

Poniatowski replied that Third Division's headquarters had considered some sort of rescue action, but he added that the Third had other things to do. As Mary Walsh put it, 'We began to understand that to the US Army Lieutenant Jack Hemingway was merely one of tens of thousands of Allied wounded captives.'

But Hemingway, who hadn't lived in the real world for years, wouldn't give up. He awoke next morning with hundreds of plans instantly hatched in his fertile brain. 'I can't go over there,' he announced. 'If the Krauts learned of it they might put the bite on Bumby [his nickname for his son]. But you could,' he added, indicating Mary. 'You're an innocent *Time* reporter. You could go and check and see if there's anything we don't know now and reconnoitre and find out some true gen.'

Mary said, adopting the tough talk she knew the writer liked, 'I can't speak any Kraut. Send Marlene.' She meant Marlene Dietrich, whom Hemingway always called 'the Kraut'.

The mind boggles at the thought of the screen vamp with the million-dollar legs reconnoitring the front line. But Hemingway didn't seem to think the suggestion absurd. Still, he wanted Mary to go, although naturally she wouldn't 'be any good behind the lines'. 'But you could talk to Bumby's outfit. Poniatowski [who had wisely slipped away] is only one of them. And to his general. You've got many friends who are generals.'

In the end Hemingway convinced her. They dreamed up a pretext for her to visit the Vosges area where Jack had disappeared. Mary was to go there to write a story on the Japanese-American 422nd Infantry Regiment. The Nisei, as these first generation Japanese-Americans were called, had recently arrived from Italy, where they had won more medals than any other American outfit, to become part of the 36th Texas Division. Her boss, Charles Wertenbaker, approved and off she went to find the 422nd and the missing Jack. She found neither. Colmar, where Jack was in hospital, was on the far side of the Vosges and the town wouldn't be captured until 1945. As for the Nisei, they were already beginning an action which would lead to their near extinction. They had no time for lady correspondents.

On that same 8 October when the *Jagdkommando* shot the eight SAS, Colonel-General Jodl presented details of the draft plan for the top-secret offensive which Hitler had dreamed up at the height of the September crisis. He told the Führer that he could provide thirty-two divisions, twelve of them panzer or panzer-grenadier, for the coming counter-attack. All of them would be fully equipped and probably motorized, thanks to the efforts of the man whom Hitler regarded as a fellow artist and spiritual son, Albert Speer. It was a tremendous achievement, an act of technical genius, a gift from the hard-pressed German people. Hitler didn't know that many of the workers who were employed by Speer to make those weapons were nothing better than slave labourers.

The man who was to send these new weapons and men streaming into the Rhineland and the West Wall was no artist, but he was some kind of military genius. His overall superior, von Rundstedt, thought little of his new subordinate. Contemptuously he called him the '*Bubimarschall*' (the boy marshal). But Field Marshal Walter Model was the kind of officer who Hitler liked. Admittedly he looked like one of the hated Prussian *Monokelfritzen* as Hitler called the monocled Prussian aristocrats who ran his armies. But he wasn't one of them, though he did sport a monocle.

Four times Model had saved the Russian front from disaster. Once he had personally led a rifle company in a counter-attack to gain lost ground. Ruthless, unscrupulous, unconcerned with politics, a hard-drinking soldier through and through, he was feared by his officers whom he rode very hard and respected by his soldiers, who thought of him as a 'front swine' like themselves.

Once in January, 1942, when the German Ninth Army had reached the end of its tether under severe Russian pressure, Model had appeared at the Ninth's HQ. Without ceremony he stalked over to the situation map on the wall, stared hard at it for a moment, then commented calmly, 'Rather a mess.' Then he started rapping out orders for an immediate counter-attack. The staff officers stared at him in amazement. Where was he going to get the troops he needed for this offensive, they asked themselves.

Finally Colonel Blaurock, Ninth Army's Chief-of-Staff, asked, 'And what, *Herr General*, have you brought us for this operation?'

Model regarded his new Chief-of-Staff calmly through his monocle and answered in one word, '*Myself!*'

Now the man who was to lead the counter-attack in the Ardennes in November (in fact it would be postponed till December) knew he had to husband his resources. That was Hitler's order. The West Wall would be held by his 'Christmas Tree' soldiers, second-rate troops, *Volksturm*, 'stomach and eye' battalions and the like. His first class assault troops could not be squandered on local counter-attacks. There were two exceptions to this: Aachen on his left flank and the Hurtgen Forest to the centre of his line.

Aachen still held. A couple of thousand second-rate troops, stiffened by a handful of SS from the Adolf Hitler Bodyguard Division, were holding against the US 30th Division, making them pay for every inch of ground.

It was no different in the Hurtgen Forest south of Aachen. Here on 16 October when the US Ninth Division was replaced, utterly exhausted, it had suffered 4,500 casualties. Together with non-battle casualties the total grew to exactly one third of the Division, for a gain of exactly 3,000 yards! It was estimated that it had cost the Ninth one fatality for every yard of ground gained.

It was followed by the 28th, which would suffer similar casualties. Sergeant Mack Morris of *Yank* magazine wrote afterwards: 'The forest will bear the scars of our advance long after our scars have healed. . . . The forest will stink of death long after the last body has been removed. For the Hurtgen was agony and there was no glory in it except the glory of courageous men.'

So Model husbanded his resources, defending the rugged terrain of the Eifel with the minimum number of men, rarely using his armour, which would soon spearhead the attack westwards. Not that they were needed, for the *Amis* were attacking in terrain where they could not use their tanks or their aerial superiority. But there was one fly in the ointment – General Balck's Army Group G on his left flank. If either Patton's Third or Patch's Seventh turned that flank and got behind the Wall they would jeopardize the whole plan, which envisaged a three-army strike on a very narrow front, some ninety kilometres broad. It would be a bold thrust by the armour for the River Meuse and then on to Antwerp, thus splitting the Anglo-American armies. But in order to carry out such a daring operation, Model required stability and security on the southern shoulder of the thrust. The four-division-strong Seventh Army under General Brandenberger was to establish a blocking position on the flank of the two armies to prevent any thrust getting very far from the south.

But what if the Americans turned the southern flank *before* the operation started?

It was a problem that gave the Field Marshal plenty of headaches while he planned for the great operation to come. Could Balck hold the Americans in the south with his ragtag Army Group? Indeed he had just written to Jodl on 10 October saying, 'Never have I commanded such motley and badly equipped troops.'

Model need not have worried. Patton, at least, had his hands full at Fort Driant and Metz. There was nothing to fear from that quarter.

★   ★   ★

'Another counter-attack,' one company commander of Yuill's 11th Regiment signalled desperately, 'and we are sunk.' By now some of the Fifth Division's men had penetrated the tunnels, groping their way blindly along them, shouting their names to identify themselves to their trigger-happy comrades at the entrances. These men in the tunnels worked, as the *Stars and Stripes* put it, like 'moles with modern equipment. Acetylene torches were brought into use to cut through steel doors and piled-up metal debris in the corridors. Demolition explosions reverberated through the subterranean chambers. Men became seriously sick from carbide fumes and had to be taken out.'

Patton, realistic enough to realize he was going nowhere at Fort Driant, sent General Gay up to sort out the situation. There he was told that 'the jig is up'. The Fifth's Assistant Divisional Commander stated, 'Further attacks within the fort would be far too costly in my opinion. Driant must be surrounded, the enemy all driven underground and destroyed there. We need four more battalions for this.'

Gay rejected the suggestion out of hand. After ten costly days the third failed attack on Fort Driant was brought to an end. The Germans had beaten Patton.

Now Patton dismissed Metz from his plans. Up to now he had fought the campaign without any real overall plan, taking the opportunities presented to him by the changing tactical situation and developing them 'on the hoof', as it were. Now for the first time in three months' campaigning Patton's staff sat down and worked out a formal plan of attack. It envisaged an infantry attack to south and north of Metz, opening the way for the Tenth Armored to roll to Saarburg on the Moselle just below the city of Trier, while his other armoured division, 'the Fighting Four', headed for the Saar below Metz towards Saareguemines and from there, with luck, on to the Rhine.

On 19 October Patton wrote a personal letter to Bradley outlining the plan and maintaining that once his infantry had destroyed the thin line of German defenders, 'the Third Army stood a good chance of penetrating the West Wall and driving rapidly to the Rhine.' The tone was no longer so pugnacious as in September when he had boasted he'd go through the Siegfried Line 'like shit through a goose'. But still it was confident.

Three days later Bradley motored down to Patton's new HQ in Nancy to discuss the planned new offensive. Bradley was sceptical. He wondered whether Patton had the resources to pull it off. Patton conceded that ammunition was short, but he maintained that if Bradley's Army Group pooled its ammunition resources, ie gave *him* ammunition from Bradley's other two armies, he would be able to jump off within forty-eight hours – and he would win.

Bradley wasn't in favour. 'I'd rather wait,' he said, 'until we all can jump off together.' Again it was that fatal Broad Front Strategy of Eisenhower's at work. All his armies would move together, but nowhere were they strong enough to strike a decisive blow against the West Wall and break through before it was too late. So Bradley left with the promise that he, Patton, would be able to resume his offensive, 'on or after 5 November'.

So Patton was left to kick his heels impotently. He travelled to have lunch and receive a medal from the sickly 'King of England', as he called him. He visited spots he had known in the 'Old War', especially where he had been wounded (it always embarrassed him that he had been shot in the backside). He entertained visiting firemen, including Marlene Dietrich, who explained that Maurice Chevalier had been cleared of collaboration with the Germans because he had only once sung to French POWs in a German stalag – without pay.* But there was still trouble for Edith Piaf, who had taken a German lover during the Occupation. Piaf would later justify her conduct in her typical cheeky manner by stating, 'My cunt might have belonged to a German, but my heart always belonged to France.' She got away with it. And in the closed circle of his admiring staff he would constantly say bitterly, 'Our whole trouble is that we don't really have a Supreme Commander'.

---

* Chevalier was notoriously mean.

3

BANZAI!

The 36th Texas Division of Patch's Seventh Army had kicked off its attack on the key road centre in the Vosges on 15 October. The Division was exceptionally strong; in addition to its own three regiments it had the support of what was the most unusual regiment in the Seventh Army, the 442nd Nisei. Bruyeres, the road centre, looked easy pickings.

These little Japanese-Americans from the West Coast and Hawaii, who had already fought valiantly in Italy, had no reason to risk their lives for the United States. Back in 1941 after that 'Day of Infamy' when the Japanese had launched their surprise attack on Pearl Harbor, they were subjected to great humiliation and even physical abuse. Those who had already been drafted into the US Army in 1940 were summarily dismissed.

Royal Manaka of the 442nd remembered, 'Every time I heard that my country is the land of liberty it used to make me cry. It was not the land of the free because they took my parents and relatives and put them in a camp.' Many of those who would serve America so bravely were in a similar situation, their parents ejected from their homes in a matter of hours and transported to remote barren camps where they lived in shacks under guard for months, even years.

Eventually they were allowed to volunteer for the US Army straight from the internment camps. In the end some 4,500 did, of whom 9,500 became casualties (that is, including replacements), winning 18,000 individual medals for bravery. But even in battle, the men of the 'Go For Broke'* outfit were bitter and resentful. As one man told Royal Manaka, 'He said not to send him back to the States if he was killed because he

---

* A Hawaiian Nisei gambling term which became the regimental motto.

had no home to go to where he could be buried.' That soldier was killed in the Vosges and was buried in France, where he remains to this day.

With their combination of that complicated blend of Japanese honour, the *Bushido* code, and American patriotism, they had been a great combat success in Italy. As one of them, Don Seki, who lost an arm in the Vosges, recalled long afterwards, 'Our forefathers believed in country, parents and relatives. We didn't want to dishonor them. In the backs of our minds, we all felt we couldn't screw up.' Hank Yoshitaka remembered, 'If the word got back to your families they would never live it down.'

Now the Regiment was going into its first action in France, attached to a strange division of Texans, under the command of a general, General Dahlquist, who was an unknown quantity to them.

After two days of severe fighting a two-pronged attack by the 36th brought the Texans to the outskirts of Bruyeres, where they came under intense artillery fire from the heights above. The 442nd, supporting them, was making slower progress because it was advancing through heavily wooded hills against stiff infantry opposition. But although Bruyeres was now captured, its road network through the Vosges was of little use as long as the Germans held the surrounding hills from which they dominated the town. Someone was going to have to attack those forbidding heights.

One day after the 36th had captured Bruyeres the Nisei, who had now also entered the town, received a message from 36th Division's HQ. It read: 'General wants you to know the 442nd is not getting the publicity in *Beachhead News* [army newspaper] due to censorship. Please tell men and S-6 [Colonel Pence, the 442nd's Commander] that the General appreciates their efforts and regrets censorship does not permit any mention of the 442nd.'

Pence didn't reply to the message, but it was the first indication that General Dahlquist was not too happy to have it known that he had these Japanese-Americans under his command.

A little later another signal came in from 36th Division's HQ. It ordered the 442nd's 100 Battalion to move straight up the slopes of the heights dominating Bruyeres. The Nisei didn't like that one bit. They would have to march through open ground covered by both German artillery and aerial attack before they reached the cover of the trees beyond. Slowly it started to dawn on them that General Dahlquist regarded them as expendable.

Still, guided by a handful of Maquis, they advanced and dug in on the high ground, only to find themselves surrounded by the Germans on three sides. As one Nisei who survived wrote: 'We wait for the inevitable. The Germans have us just where they want us.'

The 'inevitable' happened. The Germans attacked from all three directions. 'The slaughter begins. It starts from the forward position. Like a slithery snake it weaves to the right, then to the left, each time moving closer to where we are . . . and as it comes nearer and nearer our trench, my gunner and I are grateful that we dug our hole under a large rock. . . . After the barrage there is an eerie kind of silence. . . . As expected many are wounded seriously, a few are buried in their slit trenches. A grotesque sight catches my eye. A shattered hand and arm is embedded on a branch halfway up a tall pine tree and it's waving at me. It sends chills up my spine and makes me want to vomit. Our worst imaginations when we first entered the Vosges forests have come true. Trees with human parts. Humans with tree parts.'

There was worse to come for the Nisei of the 100th. They had advanced a mile from the nearest other outfit of the 36th. The trail over which they had entered the forest had been cut by the Germans who had tapped into the Nisei's telephone cable and knew what was coming up to support them. Every supply group was ambushed. Ammunition started to run low. The Nisei was forced to use whatever ammunition they could find on their own dead and those of the enemy. They radioed their position to the rear. An armoured force carrying supplies, with Nisei infantrymen riding on the decks of the Shermans, was sent out to help them. It didn't get far. The Germans were waiting. Fire poured into the tanks as they rumbled up the trail. Rockets from the German *Panzerfaust* launchers zapped lethally at the Shermans. The infantry were scythed off the decks of the tanks. Sergeant Itsumu Sasaoka was critically wounded. Still he continued firing, blood pouring down his shattered body till the tanks had passed the site of the ambush. He fell from the deck of the tank into the bushes. Later when the tanks were forced to turn back, the surviving Nisei tried in vain to find the brave NCO. Later he was sighted in a German POW camp and was reported to have been killed by the Russian 'allies' in 1945. He became yet another Nisei to be awarded a posthumous DSC.

On 22 October the 100th signalled General Dahlquist's HQ: 'The 100th will have to be throwing stones if they don't get any ammo.' That message was followed by another some time later stating; 'We are getting some enemy action from the rear. Will probably have to use the cooks pretty soon. Colonel Singles [the C.O.] wants you to know that the area is too big. Being hit from three sides.'

That day some supplies did reach the trapped battalion. They were carried on men's backs. Jeeps simply couldn't work their way through the shattered forest and the German ambushes which covered every trail. Now General Dahlquist ordered the 100th to attack the small farming community of Biffontaine. The Nisei's officers could not see any value in taking the place and they were worried that down in the valley they would be beyond the range of artillery support and out of radio range. But orders were orders. They swarmed down the steep hills and took Biffontaine. The battalion involved was immediately cut off. House to house fighting followed. 'Surrender,' the Germans only yards away yelled. 'Surrender, you are surrounded!'

'Go to hell,' the Nisei yelled back in English and Japanese.

That day a number of wounded Nisei were captured by the Germans. One of them, Stanley Akita, was put through the usual interrogation by his captors who obviously thought that a Japanese should be fighting on their side; after all Japan was Germany's ally. 'How come you're fighting for America?' Akita was asked. 'Because I'm American,' he answered stoutly. The German looked at the slant-eyed prisoner and said, 'What makes you feel like an American?' 'Because I was born in America,' Akita answered.

That day the survivors were relieved. They returned to their pup tents to the rear, men with feet swollen from trenchfoot, and found that the Quartermaster Corps had a surprise for them. Ever since the Nisei had entered the service there had been a problem finding boots and uniforms of the right size for them. Most of the Nisei were much smaller and slighter than the average GI. Now at the town of Belmont to the rear the Quartermaster Service dumped a huge supply of clothing for them to pick whatever they wanted. The Nisei stared at the new gear in disbelief. The sizes were right, but the clothing was intended for the US Army's female auxiliaries, the WACs! Khaki-coloured knickers and bras weren't exactly their style. So in the end they took the WAC raincoats; they fitted nicely. But there were still no boots, the infantryman's most basic piece of equipment.

One day after the relief of the 100th Dahlquist's 141st Infantry was ordered to move forward. Less than an hour after moving off the lead battalion, the First, was in trouble and the trouble apparently did not come only from the Germans. As the Journal of the 442nd recorded for that day: 'The 141st is having trouble up there. What they thought were Maquis are not Maquis but Miliciens. So warn all your outfits if they [the Frenchmen] should make any act of hostility just shoot, and try to get prisoners because we'd like to get some information. . . . The 100th had reported some Frenchmen being not so civil. . . . These Miliciens are French collaborators and very dangerous. There are no Maquis now. They have all been called back and disbanded.'

Naturally the news that the French were fighting on the side of the Germans in the Vosges was censored. In a month's time men of Patch's Third Division would discover the concentration camp at Natzweiler, the only one on French soil. Then, of course, the publicity machine would crack into action to detail this evidence of National Socialist brutality. What would not be revealed was that most of the camp's four thousand inmates had been delivered to the concentration camp by the French themselves! The SS might well have done the torturing and exterminating, but it had been the French who had provided them with their victims.

★   ★   ★

The military defeat in 1940 had seemed to many millions of Frenchmen proof of the perfidy of the corrupt politicians of the Third Republic who had taken France into this disastrous war with Germany. France's defeat was only explicable by the criminal negligence of the politicians.

As a result the new Vichy Government of Unoccupied France, under the leadership of the aged Marshal Pétain, immediately donned the hairshirt and determined to cleanse French life of its corrupting influence. Pétain had once purged the broken French Army of 1917 by breaking off the senseless mass slaughter of Verdun and then decimating the ranks of the mutineers by firing squad. Now he was out to cleanse the whole of France, again with force if necessary.

Within days of taking power Pétain's government started passing anti-semitic laws. It required no spurring on by the Germans. There were plenty of anti-semites in France already. Jews were accused of having corrupted French life with their decadent art, books, movies and flashy way of life.

In a letter of devastating irony, the head of the Paris bar and ex-senator, Pierre Masse, wrote to Pétain directly after he had heard that Jews would now be barred from becoming army officers: 'I would be obliged if you would tell me what I have to do to withdraw rank from my brother, a second lieutenant in the 36th Infantry Regiment, killed at Douaumont in April, 1916; from my son-in-law, Second Lieutenant in the Dragoons, killed in Belgium in May, 1940; from my nephew J.-F. Masse, killed in

Rethel in May, 1940. Can I leave my brother his *Médaille Militaire* . . . my son, wounded in June, 1940, his rank?'

Pétain didn't reply. Irony was wasted on the aged Marshal. Masse was arrested by the French police just like the rest. He died in a concentration camp in Germany.

It was the French police who rounded up 5,000 French children of Jewish origin and handed them over to the Germans to do with what they liked. It was French detectives who arrested French resistance workers and the British agents who helped them and handed them over to the Gestapo. It was the French para-military police, the hated *Milice*, who fought pitched battles with the *Maquis* in southern France in a vain attempt to stop them aiding the advancing US Seventh Army.

Unknown to the ordinary 'dough' of the Seventh Army who was putting his life on the line every day in order to 'liberate' France, a goodly section of its population was totally indifferent to their being there, and a smaller number actually *hated* them for disrupting their comfortable lives.

A future president of France, Mitterand, loyally served Vichy and won its highest award until it became clear that it was a liability to have a Vichy record. A resistance record was the thing to have. So he joined the resistance. De Lattre de Tassigny, currently commanding the 1st French Army under Devers, had loyally served the Vichy government at the head of his division until the Allies landed in North Africa in November, 1942, and he saw the writing on the wall and hurriedly changed sides. Indeed de Lattre is reputed to have sworn after Britain had 'betrayed' France in 1940 that he would gladly lead his division in any German invasion of *la perfide Albion*.

Three months before D-Day, when everywhere in Southern England the massed US divisions waiting for the word to go were being lectured on the righteousness of what their Supreme Commander called 'the Crusade in Europe', one million Parisiens lined the streets of the capital to welcome a hero. It was Marshal Pétain arriving, as the head of the Vichy Government, for a state visit to the German Occupation authorities. Four years before, on the day he had assumed power, the President of the French National Assembly had told the aged Marshal that he was to attempt 'to render more austere a Republic that we had made too easy'. Now in October, 1944, here were these foreigners undoing all the Victor of Verdun's good work.

So even when it was clear that they were on the losing side, there were still some Frenchmen prepared to play an active role against the Americans, even if it meant fighting with the Germans against them.*

★   ★   ★

General Patch soon received the news that his 36th Division was not only fighting Germans but also Frenchmen. But that day, the day the 442nd was relieved and the fact was recorded in the regiment's diary, Patch's mind was elsewhere. The day before he had received devastating personal news. At six in the afternoon of 22 October, General Patch was in his office waiting to take part in the evening briefing in the War Room when he received a phone call from General Spragins, commanding the 44th Division and a close personal friend since their days at West Point. Patch took the call and then went into the War Room. He went through the evening briefing as usual and then strode out to his waiting car with his aide, Colonel Bartlett. On the way Patch said to Bartlett, 'Do you know what General Spragins had to tell me?'

Bartlett shook his head.

'He told me Mac was killed today.' Mac was his son, a captain of infantry serving in his own 79th Infantry Division. As Bartlett recorded later, Patch didn't break down, but was 'sombre for the rest of the evening'.

Immediately Patch telegraphed his wife that her son was dead and asked her to tell 'Ginger', his daughter-in-law, mother of a one-year-old child. The telegram was delivered the next morning and her daughter found Mrs Patch 'bent over queerly', with the Western Union telegram clutched in her hand. As her daughter described it afterwards, 'She turned and sort of waved the telegram and said in a funny voice, "It's Mac. Yes, dead".'

On 23 October General Spragins brought Mac's body to Patch's HQ at Epinal. He had only left the town a few days before after recovering from a wound in the shoulder. Patch didn't want anything special done for his son. He wanted him buried in a mattress cover like any other soldier. But the staff chipped in for a French carpenter to make a coffin for the dead officer. Then the body was taken out down the long tree-lined *allée* which led to the Seventh Army cemetery beyond the town. It is still there.

---

* There was even a French SS Division, the 'Charlemagne', which took part in the last defence of Berlin. Indeed the last man to win the Knight's Cross of the Iron Cross in the Second World War was a Frenchman!

The ceremony was brief and Patch kept his composure, whispering as he left the new grave, 'So long, Son'.

But in a letter he wrote to his wife that night he gave way to his emotions. He wrote: 'Oh we can be and are proud of that boy – but I do not feel embarrassed in telling you that, as I write, the tears are falling from my eyes and it is hard for me to continue. He passed away in the manner that has reflected the greatest credit upon himself, his wife and son and his mother and father and upon his country. That boy lived and died as a complete, loyal exemplification of his Alma Mater, West Point.'

★   ★   ★

But the war went on in all its deadly fury. By the time of Captain Patch's funeral at Epinal the lead elements of the Texas Division were in serious trouble. In particular the First Battalion of the 36th Division's 141st Regiment had been trapped and cut off by a sudden German attack along the ridge upon which they had been advancing. The First Battalion's Companies 'A' and 'B', part of Company 'C' and a platoon of Company 'D' were trapped with the Germans all around them. Now their only means of communication with the rear was over the radio used by the forward artillery observer, Lieutenant Erwin Blonder.

The latter reported the position of the 'Lost Battalion', as it was soon going to be known in the Seventh Army. That night the 151st's Second Battalion launched a relief attack, but its advance was blocked by superior forces west of Biffontaine, which the Nisei had captured three days before. One day later a battalion of the resting 442nd Regiment was ordered up to take over the positions of the 3rd Battalion of the 151st so that they could assault the German besiegers. It also failed.

Now the trapped men had to hang on as best they could until some means was found of getting through to them. In all there were 275 GIs spread out in foxholes over an area of some 300 yards, with, as they signalled that night over the artillery officer's radio, 'No rations, no water, no communications with headquarters, four litter cases.' Around them there were approximately 700 Germans.

Disorganized at first, and knowing now there was going to be no early relief for them, they started to prepare for a long defence. Four officers, all lieutenants, formed an 'advisory council', with 1st Lieutenant Martin Higgins, the most experienced, having the final say.

They ordered the defences put in order and then asked for a 'shake down'. Everyone had to empty his pack so that anything they had could be shared. Everything was collected from small stoves and petrol to precious chocolate bars. But water was in desperately short supply. Finally a dirty water hole was found on the side of the hill. The water was stagnant and it could only be fetched in the middle of the night because the German besiegers were using the same puddle, but it was water.

'We used to talk about food mostly,' one of the trapped men of the 'Lost Battalion', Sergeant William Bandorick, recalled afterwards. 'We talked about chocolate cakes and bacon and eggs and everything that our mothers and wives used to make for us back home. I remember once we spent a whole afternoon just talking about flapjacks, golden brown with butter.'

For five days the trapped men starved. Some grubbed for wild mushrooms. It was the season for such things. Others attempted to trap small birds. Some searched their uniforms and packs for hours for some small crumb of something edible which they had overlooked during the shakedown. But there was no food at all.

There was no talk of surrender either. Any time Higgins asked for volunteers for patrols, he had the pick of the whole Battalion. But the patrols didn't get far. Once a 36–man strong patrol walked straight into a German ambush. Five men got back to the trapped companies. One, Private Horace Male, got through the Germans and wandered about the forest for five days until he was picked up by the patrols of the 3rd Battalion.

Desperately the 36th Division's artillery tried to supply the Battalion with shells normally used for firing propaganda leaflets into German lines. These shells the artillerymen filled with D-rations and aid packs. But the idea wasn't too successful. The shells buried themselves too deep into the ground or burst in the tree tops, scattering the precious rations for the Germans to pick up when they wanted.

On the fifth day of the siege General Dahlquist asked for air support from the XII AAC Air Force. He wanted them to use their P-47 fighter bombers to drop supplies to his beleaguered troops. The 'birdmen', as they were called by the infantry, agreed. On the hillside hurried preparations were made to receive the aerial drop. The GIs chipped in their underwear to make a long white arrow to mark their positions on the hillside. To make doubly sure, they attached smoke grenades to saplings above their foxholes. Once the planes appeared they would pull out the pins and release the smoke.

The first attempt fell a hundred yards short of the hilltop. The men moaned in dismay. All morning their stomachs had been rumbling in anticipation. The P-47s came round in tight curves, ignoring the German tracer zipping up at them from the ground.

'We were just praying, that's all,' recalled Sergeant Howard Jessup. 'We just sat in our foxholes, listening hard, not saying a word, and we just prayed.'

And their prayers were answered. The fighter-bombers dropped their belly tanks full of the precious goodies accurately this time and for the first time since they had been trapped by the Germans the men ate. They could loosen their belts, replete at last. But they couldn't relax. They were still cut off.

4

THE LOST BATTALION

The Nisei kicked off their attack at three o'clock on the morning of 26 October. The actual distance between their start line and the hilltop position of the Lost Battalion was a mere four miles. But as the Germans had parts of the forested hillsides mined and had observation posts everywhere, the Nisei would have to detour and outflank German positions time and again, so the real distance they would have to cover would be twice that.

Three battalions abreast, each man with a sheet of white toilet paper pinned to his back for identification purposes, they slipped through the trees, sloshing through the mud of the steep trails. The Germans were waiting for them of course. Their trap was well baited with the Lost Battalion and the enemy knew that the *Amis* would try again to free their trapped comrades.

But the Nisei plodded onwards doggedly in temperatures down to freezing and with fog shrouding the tops of the hills. Each man searched the area immediately to his front for the sight of a German. One of the first messages sent back by the advancing battalions at just after seven that morning stated, 'It's so dark that you can't see a hand in front of your face. I don't want to walk blindly into them.'

But the Germans, well accustomed to fighting in dense forests – they had had plenty of experience of it in Russia – didn't give their positions away by firing at the Nisei as they advanced. They waited until the Japanese-Americans had slogged by them up the forest trail and then they opened up at their backs from the flanks.

Now the battle started to warm up. The first bursts of machine-gun fire were followed by the howls of *Nebelwerfers*. Thick trails of black smoke hissed into the sky. A moment later barrages of 105mm shells from the electrically powered mortars came falling from above. Firs snapped like matchsticks. Men staggered to a sudden halt. The Nisei started to take casualties.

Tanks were whistled up, but they were of little value to the infantry in the tight confines of the forest. And the Germans were prepared for them. Soldiers armed with the German one-shot rocket launcher crept through the trees. A flash of scarlet flame, the hollow boom of metal striking metal and the first Sherman was knocked out.

Desperately engineers, under the command of Captain Pershing Nakada (he was named 'Pershing' by his father who had served as General Pershing's orderly in the First World War), felled firs and spruce to make a corduroy road so that more tanks could be brought up. But it was beginning to grow dark again and the infantry commanders knew it was no use trying to go any further in the gloom. They ordered their men to dig in. With luck the mess sergeants might be able to get some warm food up to the frozen, weary infantry.

The men started to doze off. There was no sound now save the breeze in the trees and the permanent barrage a long way off. As Sergeant Stanley Nakamoto of the 100th Battalion recalled long afterwards: 'It was so quiet. And the Germans were letting us alone so my men dozed off. Suddenly I heard Germans talking! I crawled and saw them coming up the hill and I grabbed my tommy gun and began shooting. . . . When my boys began shooting, the Jerries must have thought it was a whole company so they took off.'

Doggedly the Nisei set off once more on the following morning, their breath coming in gasps as they laboured up yet another hill. They started coming across the first dead Texans, crumpled in their foxholes like bundles of khaki rags. There were Germans too, but these were live ones, filtering through the trees. The Nisei opened up and flung grenades. The Germans fled back to the cover of the deep forest and, as Sergeant Nakamoto remarked, 'I think the Germans knew then that the Japanese soldiers were on the line. They were afraid of us, you know. They didn't counter-attack that time.'

Now General Dahlquist started to take a hand in the operation. As the Nisei began to slow down again due to heavy enemy resistance and the Nisei's third battalion, under the command of Lieutenant-Colonel James Hanley, left the regiment to head for Hill 617 where he hoped to spring a trap on the Germans, he signalled to Colonel Pence: 'Get the men out of there *crawling*, and get the Krauts out of the holes!'

Again Colonel Pence realized that for Dahlquist his men were cannon fodder. He wanted his Texans rescued, cost what it may in the lives of the Nisei. But he kept his temper and got on with the job, for he knew the Lost Battalion wouldn't be able to hold out much longer.

He was right. On that day Lieutenant Higgins, the senior officer in the Lost Battalion, was writing a letter to his wife when he suddenly signed off, 'Time out for a while, Marge. I've got work to do.'

It was more than work. This was the strongest attack the Germans had put in so far. This time they were determined to eradicate the American strongpoint behind their line. The hilltop position was swamped by the heaviest artillery bombardment the men had ever experienced.

Then they came, shouting and yelling. Fortunately they picked the one sector of the Texans' perimeter where Higgins had concentrated most of the Lost Battalion's machine guns. At first the men manning the .5 inch heavy machine guns just fired single shots. They knew that there was a shortage of ammunition and they had been ordered not to waste ammunition until they had a really good target. Now with the Germans only yards off, they really cut loose, hosing the attackers with their fire.

'We weren't firepowering, we were collecting,' Higgins recalled after the war. 'The collection was phenomenal. The Germans took an awful beating. In the fringes and brush just where the forest ended there were dozens and dozens of dead Germans.'

Higgins called down his own artillery on to the perimeter by means of that precious radio which they could use only twice a day now in order not to run the battery down. Minutes later the whole of the divisional artillery thundered into action. As Higgins said afterwards, 'The artillery made a fine collection too, spraying the whole area with tree bursts when the Germans left their covered holes. The artillery accounted for one pile which had two hundred and fifty German stiffs in it.'

The defenders had beaten off yet another attack. But their number was getting fewer and fewer. Would they manage to beat off the next one?

★   ★   ★

On 29 October General Dahlquist began to interfere more and more in the attack. On the phone repeatedly to 442nd HQ he ordered, 'Keep the Nisei going and don't let them stop. There's a battalion about to die up there and we've got to reach them.'

Fifteen minutes later the General was on the phone again: 'Keep them going. Even against opposition.'

Captain Pershing Nakada swore when he heard of that second order. He said later that no one in the Nisei regiment respected Dahlquist. 'He didn't give a damn how many people were killed as long as we just got up there.'

Then the General took his jeep up to the front to give his orders personally to the fighting officers. He tackled Lieutenant Ohata, a much-decorated veteran of the Italian campaign, that afternoon. The General asked him how many men he had left and the latter replied, 'One company, sir.'

'That's enough,' Dahlquist said and launched into the way Ohata should attack. 'Here's what you do,' he said. 'We've got to get onto that hill and across it. You get all the men you have and charge straight up the hill with fixed bayonets. That's the only way we can get the Krauts off it.'

'You want my men to charge straight up the hill, sir?' Ohata queried politely, his face revealing nothing.

'Straight up. It's the quickest way. There's a battalion going to die if we don't get to it.'

'You realize what this means for our men, sir? They'll be slaughtered going up that hill in the face of heavy fire in full daylight.'

'It's got to be done,' Dahlquist insisted.

Ohata shook his head firmly, knowing the risks he took as a humble lieutenant squaring up to a major general. 'I refuse to accept your order. You can court-martial me. You can strip me of my rank and decorations, but I refuse to accept your order.'

Dahlquist's face flushed angrily. 'You *refuse!*' he bellowed. 'I'm *ordering* you take your men and make a bayonet charge up that hill and get those Krauts off it quick.'

Ohata shook his head. 'We'll get them off *our* way,' he said stubbornly, 'and try to save as many men as possible.'

The General was dumbfounded. He walked away without another word. Ohata took the hill *his* way. Nothing more was heard of the matter.

It seemed on that fourth day of the Nisei's attempt to break through to the Lost Battalion that General Dahlquist was losing his nerve. He was here, there and everywhere behind the immediate front, threatening, pleading, cajoling. Once he ordered his artillery to fire a support mission for the 442nd. When the artillery officers checked the co-ordinates they found that their shells would have landed directly on the Texans' positions!

On that dreadful 29 October, with the Nisei taking casualties for every inch of ground they took, Dahlquist came to the CP of Colonel Alfred

Pursall, commanding the Nisei's 3rd Battalion. Again he ordered the Colonel to make his men fix bayonets and charge. Pursall would have none of it. Angrily he replied, 'Those are my boys you're trying to kill. You're not going to kill my boys. I won't let you kill my boys. If there's any orders to be given to my boys to attack, I'll give them personally and I'll lead them.' Tempers were getting frayed.

That day Colonel Pence was wounded on the ridge line and had to be evacuated, the bodies of his dead Nisei littering both sides of the trail as they brought him down. It was not surprising that years later Colonel Pence would shake with rage whenever he heard Dahlquist's name and that one of his then battalion commanders, the future Brigadier General Singles, refused publicly to shake Dahlquist's hand at a full dress review at Fort Bragg.

★　　★　　★

Still the slaughter went on. They assaulted what later became known as 'Banzai Hill'. But Colonel Pursall's Third Battalion had suffered so many casualties that they didn't yell. They didn't want to alert the Germans until they were in among them. The first attempt was made with the aid of tanks and failed. They simply could not cope with the trees, the mines and other obstacles. So the harassed Colonel was forced to do the attack with what was left of his weary infantry. He drew his pearl-handled 45, à la Patton, out of his holster, Sergeant Chet Tanaka, cowering in his foxhole, watched him and wondered if the battalion commander was going to attack all by himself. He came over to Tanaka's foxhole, looked down at him and said, 'Let's get going, Sergeant.'

Tanaka hesitated. Then he thought, 'My God, if that dumb son-of-a-bitch is going to walk up into that fire I guess we'd better go too.'

'I called to the sixteen men of 'K' Company [all that were left] to get up and get going. I was the first up, slowly. Then the others got up. We fired from our hips. No yelling. Pursall led the way.'

It was in this attack that Private Barney Hajiro was recommended for the Congressional Medal of Honor for his bravery. He went up Banzai Hill, fighting a one-man war. He knocked out two machine-gun posts, killed two snipers and generally blazed a lethal path for those who were following.

Naturally the recommendation was downgraded to the DSC, like all the other recommendations for the CMH for the Nisei. After all, how would it look if a Japanese-American received the country's top award when Japanese soldiers were committing such terrible atrocities in the

Far East? But British observers with the US Seventh Army had witnessed Private Hajiro's bravery. They submitted their own recommendation to the British War Office. Four years later Private, now Mr Hajiro, was awarded the British Military Medal for 'three separate actions in Eastern France in which he had showed gallantry under fire'. How strange that a Japanese-American should be awarded a British order for gallantry. Again the attendant publicity was minimal.

In that bold charge up Banzai Hill Company 'I' suffered five killed and forty wounded. Company 'K' was left with seventeen riflemen. All its officers were killed or wounded and Sergeant Tanaka was now the Company Commander. Indeed one battalion of 442nd was down now to two platoons. The dead and wounded were piled like cordwood on the trucks which took them to the rear. If they didn't break through soon, there'd be nothing left of the 442nd Infantry Regiment.

$$\star \quad \star \quad \star$$

30 October dawned cold and wet. There was snow in the air in the Vosges. The 442nd pushed on, but they were losing men and as their chaplain, Masao Yamada, wrote that day, 'I am spiritually low for once. My heart weeps for our men, especially those who gave all. Never has any combat affected me so deeply as this emergency mission. I am probably getting soft, but to me the price is too costly for our men. I feel this way more because the burden is laid on the combat team when the rest of the 141st is not forced to take the same responsibility.' Again the same hint that Dahlquist was sacrificing the Nisei who weren't really part of the Texas Division.

But on that cold day there was nothing that the Nisei could do about it. They had their orders and they were going to carry them out. Just after two that afternoon they sent a signal back to Division, 'Unconfirmed. They think they have the first traces of the Lost Battalion. They have passed the road block and are going up the hill.'

Two hours later Sergeant Edward Guy of the Lost Battalion was on outpost duty when he saw something moving in the afternoon gloom. *Germans!* He strained his eyes. But could Germans be that small? Then, as the Divisional History puts it, 'He raced down the hill like crazy, yelling and laughing and grabbing the lone soldier.' That lone soldier, Private Mutt Sakumoto, just looked at him, a lump in his throat. All he could think of to say was, 'Do you guys need any cigarettes?'

The Nisei had linked up with the Lost Battalion at last. But the cost had been great. In four days the 442nd had suffered 117 killed, 657 wounded and forty missing to rescue 211 Texans, all that were left of the original 275 caught in the trap. In the 442nd's 3rd Battalion, Company 'K' was down to seventeen riflemen and Company 'I' had only eight left. Both companies were commanded by sergeants.

In the US War Department's later biographical sketch of General Dahlquist it is stated, 'This was the first time in military history that this portion of the Vosges Mountains had ever been successfully attacked.' Some of the success of that assault was undoubtedly made possible by the despised Nisei, who even after the war was over still had to suffer in the United States due to their race.

As an 18-year-old Dan Inonya, who would one day become a United States Senator, had volunteered for the Army from his native Hawaii. He had been in the thick of the fighting in Italy and then in France, where he had won the Distinguished Service Cross at the cost of losing his right arm. That meant an end to his ambition to become a doctor. In the summer of 1945 he returned home, his chest ablaze with ribbons, his empty sleeve pinned to an immaculate tunic. At his San Francisco stopover while he waited for transport to Hawaii to see his family for the first time in two years, he decided to get his hair cut. He went into the nearest barbershop. The barber looked at him coldly in the big mirror beyond the chair. He took in the dark skin and slant eyes. He turned and gestured angrily with his razor, snapping, 'We don't serve Japs here.'

5

THE LIMEYS TAKE A HAND

In the first week of November, while Patch and Patton prepared for new attacks in the south and Hodges was still bogged down in the middle of the front in the Hurtgen Forest, 'Big Simp' Simpson, Commander of the US Ninth Army to the north invited the nearest British Corps Commander to dinner to meet Ike.

General Brian Horrocks, 'Jorrocks' as he was universally known in the British Army, the commander of the British XXX Corps, accepted with alacrity. 'Jorrocks', an ascetic-looking general, who had seen more than enough of war – he had been wounded in both wars and had been a POW of both the Germans and the Russians – had never met Ike informally. Besides he knew that American generals lived in some style, something frowned upon by Montgomery, who always took sandwiches with him when he went to visit US headquarters so that he didn't have to eat their food.

'Big Simp', who kept his head shaved – Patton said of him, 'When he's not fighting he works as an advertisement for a hair restorer' – welcomed his visitor effusively and ushered him into the dining room where Ike and his chief of staff, 'Beetle' Smith, were already seated.

After the recent losses XXX Corps had suffered trying to reach the trapped British 1st Airborne Division at Arnhem, Montgomery had warned Horrocks not to get involved in any more offensive actions for the time being. But neither Montgomery nor his Corps Commander had reckoned with the Supreme Commander's charm.

After an excellent dinner, Eisenhower asked, 'Well, Jorrocks, are you going to take on Geilenkirchen for us?' Geilenkirchen was the largest German town in the area where the US Ninth and the British Second Armies linked up.

Horrocks replied that the spirit was willing, but the flesh was weak.

The only division he had available was the veteran 43rd Infantry, which had already suffered tremendous casualties. Behind his back the men of the 43rd called their Commanding General 'Butcher Thomas', and by the time the campaign ended the Division would have had a complete turnround in strength, due to some 12,500 casualties in all. With that one division Horrocks didn't think he could take Geilenkirchen, one of the strongest positions on the northern wing of the West Wall.

'Give him one of ours, Simp,' Eisenhower said to the Army Commander.

'Big Simp' suggested the 84th Infantry, a green division which had recently arrived from the States.

Horrocks protested that the task ahead was going to be very difficult and it didn't seem fair to launch a US division into its first battle under the command of a British general.

But Simpson and Eisenhower overrode his protestations. So the conversation continued, Eisenhower expressing his anger at the conduct of the 82nd and 101st Airborne Divisions which had been withdrawn from Holland and were now in France. There had been a lot of drunkenness, several score desertions and some rapes. At one time Eisenhower had considered having public executions of rapists to show the French populace that the American authorities meant business. 'They are a disgrace to the whole US Army,' Eisenhower said.

Thereupon Horrocks, who had fought side by side with those same divisions back in September during the Arnhem operation, told Eisenhower that it was a shame that the whole of the US Army didn't consist of such 'disgraces'.

Horrocks's angry sally brought a roar of laughter from Smith. He commented, 'Well, well, I never thought I'd hear a Britisher standing up for US troops against an American general.'

So it was, in the framework of Eisenhower's Broad Front Strategy (or the lack of it), that an Anglo-American formation was scheduled to attack the West Wall.

In that first week of November the two divisions regrouped in order to be in the most favourable position for their attack on the West Wall at Geilenkirchen. There was the usual good-natured badinage whenever they met. 'Where yer been since 1939, Yank?' 'Waiting for the order to come over here and save you, Limey.' To the British the Americans were thought of as 'overfed, over-paid, over-sexed and *over here.*' To the Americans, the British were a slow-moving, class-ridden bunch who downed tools and drank tea at the drop of a hat.

But in fact the class-conscious British officers took more care of their soldiers than the supposedly more democratic Americans. They felt it was their duty to put their men first, checking their feet daily for signs of trenchfoot, ensuring that they got fresh socks and warm food, however primitive, every day in the line. It didn't come as a surprise to the men of the 43rd Division to learn that the 84th Division suffered 500 casualties from trenchfoot in their first week in combat.

So the British moved into the sector vacated by the 84th, getting ready for the assault, only to find to their horror that the Americans had not made an accurate map of the minefields through which the 43rd would attack. Sappers were sent out immediately. They brought in 700 stray mines. But they didn't find them all. That day Brigadier Mole, commanding the 43rd Division's 129th Brigade, was inspecting his line when there was a tremendous explosion. It blew a crater thirty foot wide and five foot deep. What was left of Brigadier Mole and fourteen other British soldiers were found in and around it.

The attack would go ahead with a new brigadier, but all depended upon the weather for the aerial support they needed.

At 12.45, right on schedule, the vast bombing fleet headed for the front. The RAF and US Army Air Corps planes were to blast a path free for General Thomas's British 43rd Division and General Bolling's US 84th.

Now the guns started to thunder as the 'funnies' of the British 79th Division rumbled out into no-man's-land to clear the mines. The flails churned through the mud, beating the earth two or three yards to their front with their whirling chains and exploding the mines. After an hour they had cleared two lanes through the German minefield.

The 84th started to move out on the right flank. It was their task to take the high ground to the right of Geilenkirchen. Once that was done, the British 43rd would advance to the left. The intention was to encircle Geilenkirchen completely.

At midday two battalions of British infantry moved into the attack. The supporting tanks started to lag behind. Unlike the German tanks, Allied ones still ran on narrow tracks which made it difficult to move through thick mud. It was the same with their supply vehicles. They became hopelessly bogged down. Still the infantry plodded on. A couple of German self-propelled guns scuttled out of the woods to the right. They opened up at once before the British could react. They shot the lead platoons to ribbons. Within a matter of minutes thirty-one men lay dead. But the infantry pushed on grimly.

By nightfall both divisions had achieved their objective. The West Wall strongpoint at Geilenkirchen was surrounded. But the battle had only just begun.

That night the heavens opened. The rain poured down. It drenched the freezing infantry and turned the fields into a quagmire. And the Germans started to react. Their artillery opened up with a vengeance. For the first time the 84th Division discovered what it was like to come under a concentrated German artillery bombardment. Nevertheless, at dawn they started to attack across the sodden fields into the West Wall. They didn't get far. As the supporting Shermans began to bog down, tanks of the German 15th Panzer Division rumbled into action. The Americans went to ground. Watching the German tanks, Brigadier Essame of the 43rd thought, 'It was galling to see their tanks with broad tracks manoeuvring over muddy fields impossible to our own.'

The 43rd kept on going, but, as the historian of the Duke of Cornwall's Light Infantry wrote after the war, 'Years after the event those who survived could recall the intensity of the enemy fire and the sloppy ground over which they had to move to reach their objective. What is difficult to describe is the physical agony of the infantryman. The November rain seemed piercingly cold. After exertion when the body warmed, the cold air and the wet seemed to penetrate to the very marrow of every bone in the body so that the whole shook as with ague and a feeling of surrender to forces of nature far greater in strength than any enemy might impose.' This feeling could only be conquered by 'the inherent claim of self-preservation and the determination to do one's duty'.

Horrocks ordered the Duke of Cornwall's to resume their attack. The battalion, which had already lost one CO killed in action and would lose another before it was over, pushed on, right into a counter-attack by the 10th SS Panzer Division. All day the battle raged. They reached the village of Hoven where house-to-house fighting took place. The British avoided the village streets as best they could. Instead they 'mouse-holed' from house to house, blasting through adjoining walls or crawling through attics to confront the SS in their hideouts.

Everything now depended upon the Americans on the right flank. They had been ordered to capture the key bunkers around the village of Suggerath. If they couldn't the Duke of Cornwall's would be isolated in Hoven. Brigadier Essame, who commanded the brigade to which they belonged, was in a quandary. If the 84th didn't take their objective by dawn he would have to withdraw his battered battalion in daylight, a risky business.

While Essame wondered what he should do Horrocks appeared. He was very much a commander who led from the front. Essame told him his problem and Horrocks said he believed that the Americans could do it, but the final decision rested with Essame. He would have the Corps Commander's backing whatever he did.

Horrocks left and Essame considered the problem. Could he risk the lives of what remained of the Duke of Cornwall's? The Americans were green and this was their first battle. The Cornwalls had been fighting since June and had suffered one hundred per cent casualties in their rifle companies. As he wrote afterwards, 'The DCLI had never since the early days in Normandy fought otherwise than to the bitter end.' But could he subject them again to another blood-letting? In the end he decided he'd take a chance with the Americans.

Meanwhile Horrocks hedged his bets. He drove through the night, his staff car followed by enemy tracer. Reaching General Bolling's HQ, he said he would loan him some of his Funnies if the 84th would attack at dawn and cover the one and a half miles that separated them from his lead battalion at Hoven. Bolling promised him that the 84th would have a go.

Just before dawn the SS rushed the HQ of the Cornwall's 'D' Company, but the defenders repelled the SS grenadiers. However, a hand grenade smashed the radio and a German tank split the cable that the Cornwalls had laid under cover of darkness to the rear. 'D' Company was now isolated from the rest of the battalion.

At first light the SS came crawling up under the cover of a hedge. The men of 'D' Company rushed to their positions. For two hours the two sides battled it out. A Panther rumbled into the attack. 'D's' Company Commander seized a Piat (a primitive spring-loaded form of the bazooka with a kick like a mule). From an upstairs window he fired at the advancing tank, but the bomb bounced off the Panther's thick hide like a ping-pong ball. The German gunner fired. At that range he couldn't miss. Company Commander John Spencer fell back, severely wounded.

Another of the Battalion's companies was cut off. The cellars of the houses were packed with German and British wounded. A German doctor in the SS was captured and helped to tend the wounded. Truculently he told his captors when asked why he was fighting, 'I'm fighting for my country, the same as you.' Outside the whole of Hoven was ablaze. The defenders' ammunition ran out. Soldiers ran out and grabbed weapons and ammunition from the dead SS grenadiers sprawled in the cobbled streets. Both the remaining company commanders were wounded. Still the relieving Americans were not in sight.

The Germans brought up more tanks. Casualties started to mount alarmingly. 'D' Company was down to fifteen men out of 120. 'A' Company counter-attacked and forced the Germans back fifty yards, but again the cost was very high. The battalion, what was left of it, began to pull back. The two wounded majors refused to surrender. Instead they fought their way out of the burning village that had cost so many lives. Unknown to them, the Americans had now captured Suggerath. Not that it mattered. The steam was going out of the offensive in the north. The attack, part of Hodges' 17 Division's attack, which he had called confidently 'the last offensive necessary to bring Germany to her knees' had failed. As Brigadier Essame wrote after the war: 'Bradley, the Army Group Commander, had chosen to attack where the Germans were numerically stronger and where they had every advantage in the form of concrete defences and thick forests – a military problem new to his troops and for which they had not been trained. . . . Condemned to a battle of attrition, the infantry sustained such losses that divisions quickly exhausted themselves in action.'

Again the West Wall had beaten the Allies. They started to dig in once more and at his HQ Bradley complained to Bedell Smith, 'If the Germans would only hit us now. I'd welcome a counter-attack. We would kill many more Germans a good deal easier if they would only climb out of their holes and come after us for a change.'

They were words he would live to regret.

*   *   *

Patton, to the south, had been waiting for the rain to clear in Lorraine before he launched his two-corps attack to the north and south of Metz, which still held out stubbornly. He had received two new divisions, the 10th Armored and the 95th Infantry, and believed that once the offensive was under way he would be given the 83rd Infantry Division by Bradley. In particular, he had high hopes for Walker's XX Corps. Its 90th Division would assault the Moselle. Behind it would come the 10th Armored, driving for Saarburg. Once there, Trier would be captured and the path would be open for a drive on the Rhine fifty miles away. Behind the 10th Armored there would be the 83rd Division, which he thought Bradley would loan him from Hodges' VIII Corps, and which would establish the vital bridgehead over the River Saar, once the 10th Armored had reached Saarburg.

But the 2,000 planes he had been promised to batter the way ahead for his two corps were unable to fly. Day after day the rain came down. The attack was postponed for seventy-two hours until 8 November. On the 7th it poured down all day. Patton kept looking out of his office window at No 10 Rue d'Auxerre in Nancy. But the rain persisted.

At seven that night General Eddy, commander of his XII Corps, and General Grow, who commanded the Sixth Armored Division, came to plead with him to call off the attack on account of the rain.

'The attack will go on,' Patton said harshly, 'rain or no rain. And I'm sure it will succeed.'

When the two generals pleaded for the start to be postponed, Patton said, 'I think you'd better recommend the men you would like appointed as your successors.' That did it. They gave up.

That night Patton went to bed in full uniform. He didn't sleep too well. He was plagued by doubts. At quarter past five in the morning he was startled by the roar of 400 guns firing. It was the softening-up barrage. He slipped out of bed, hurried to the window of his bedroom and pulled back the blackout. But the dawn was dull and dismal. There would be no massive air strike to aid his offensive that day. To the east the sky flickered and trembled with the flashes of the guns. 'I thought how the enemy must have felt now that the attack he had dreaded so long had come at last,' he told an aide later.

As he stood there, the windows of his billet vibrating with the thunder of the guns, his 90th Division had begun their attack, seemingly catching the Germans by surprise as they headed for that white elephant of pre-war France, the Maginot Line.

Three-quarters of an hour later Eddy's XII Corps was also attacking with three regiments of his 80th Division in the lead, as the Germans slowly began to react to the new offensive.

At eight Bradley called from Luxemburg. 'What are your plans, George?' Bradley asked.

It was the sort of question that Patton loved. They were the kind that gave him an opportunity to surprise people. 'I'm attacking, Brad,' he answered. 'Can't you hear our guns.' He held out the phone for a moment.

'*What?*' Bradley exploded. 'You're attacking – without air support?'

Patton said he was. He had already decided to do so the night previously, even if the weather was too bad for the bombers to fly. Bradley recovered splendidly. He knew that any action Patton undertook would ensure that his Army Group and not Montgomery's would get the kudos – and the supplies – which he always craved. 'Hang on Georgie,' he said. 'Ike is here and wants to speak to you.'

'Georgie,' Eisenhower said. 'This is Ike. I'm thrilled, boy. I expect a hell of a lot from you. So carry the ball all the way.'

'Thanks General. We will, sir. We sure will.'

It was drizzling again when Patton set off with Codman to visit the CPs of three newly arrived divisions, the 44th, 100th and 103rd. That would be followed by a visit to the forward observation post of Eddy's XII Corps. By the time they reached it, the rain had stopped and the sun came out for the first time for days. With it came what Codman called 'a glorious sight': American fighter-bombers, hundreds of them, streaking across the sky eastwards to where the smoke markers indicated where the German positions were.

Patton's eyes shone. He yelled to Codman above the thunder of the guns and the roar of the planes' engines, 'I'm almost sorry for those German bastards!'

Later that day Eddy reported all was going well and all the Corps' objectives had been seized. At supper that night Patton, happy and relaxed for the first time for days, commented, 'It takes a lot out of you to prepare for such an attack and Eddy had cold feet because he was tired (Patton didn't know the fact that Eddy was keeping the secret that he was suffering from extremely high blood pressure because he didn't want to be sent back to the States). I've always maintained that there are more tired commanders than troops. But I knew he'd be all right once the show got on the road.'

That night it started to rain again.

★   ★   ★

The conditions were terrible: bitter rain, sometimes turning to snow, thick gooey mud and fog. Although the Germans were retreating slowly, they were making the Americans pay for every inch of ground. Tumbledown villages that looked as if they had not seen a lick of paint since the French Revolution were turned into strongpoints to which the Germans clung tenaciously. Not only did they provide protection against American gunfire, they also gave some shelter from the elements.

A member of the 90th Division's 357th Regiment recalls spending a night out in the open in pouring rain, longing for first light so he could have a cigarette in safety. When dawn finally came, as if reluctant to throw its light on the miserable, wartorn landscape below, 'I could make out a large haystack only a few feet away. I walked over to it and lit a smoke with my Zippo. I had filled it a few days before by dipping it into the gas tank of a jeep.'

The lighter flared up, fanned by the icy wind which was blowing across the battlefield. 'As I touched it to my cigarette I was amazed to see the side of the haystack open. Out marched four Germans, hands clasped to the tops of their helmets. They surrendered, apparently because they thought I was about to cook their camouflaged pillbox with a flame-thrower.' It was that kind of battlefield.

Michael Klemick can remember the weather that November even in his sick bed fifty years on.* 'I often wonder what was worst, the rain or the snow. It rained for days on end. It seems that there was nothing you could do to get warm again. After a while you start to smell, then you blame your buddy and then he blames you. After a while you look at your buddy and start to laugh. Laughing wasn't something that came easy, but somehow you did it anyway.'

But as the advance pushed forward painfully, with Patton's Third taking casualties all the time and the field hospitals to the rear filling up with hundreds and then thousands of wounded men, there was not much laughter to be heard on the battlefield that second week of November.

One young infantry officer of the 90th Division had spent the previous night in a foxhole sharing half a blanket with another officer and with the nearest German foxhole only 15 yards away. Towards morning it began to snow and he was glad to be ordered to report back to his battalion HQ. As he followed the telephone cable back, he reflected on the fact that at eleven o'clock on this day, 11 November, twenty-six years before, an armistice had been declared and in these same fields Germans and Americans had come out of their trenches and fraternized with each other. Now they were fighting one another again.

The young officer came level with the Battalion Aid Station. Outside there were the frozen bodies of American soldiers, eight or nine to a row, five rows deep, and all sprinkled with the night's snow. For all the world they looked like a pile of logs.

Then he caught sight of a fellow officer and friend, Joe Boyd, who had been in the thick of the fighting since Normandy. He blew his top

* In a letter to the author, 4.10.95.

at the way Joe and the rest had been treated. He stormed into the Aid Station, screaming and ranting.

'What the hell are all those bodies doing out there?' he bellowed. 'Why are they stacked up like that? Don't you know it is a terrible thing to come back here and see how little you think of us? Why haven't they been evacuated?'

He was given a slug of whisky and told by the Battalion Surgeon that for the time being only the wounded could be evacuated.

'You mean we aren't important when we die?' the young officer asked contemptuously.

A couple of officers from HQ had heard him screaming. They came in and tried to calm him down. But he wasn't having it. 'Listen if you can't get them back across the river, then get them out of my sight. If you don't I'll never come back here again nor send any of my men back. *You'll* have to come up to where *we* are if you want to see us. I mean it.'

The bodies were removed. The staff officers didn't want to risk going up front. They, too, might have ended up dead and unimportant.

So the 90th Division and the other attacking formations fought their way steadily forward. As one observer of the 90th commented on 11 November, 1944: 'The floor of the valley is mud, thick mud. The GIs are slowly plodding across, some staggering under the weight of mortars and machine guns. Shells are falling all around them, but the men do not even drop to the ground to protect themselves. The reason is the shells are burying themselves in the mud. When they explode they throw mud and fragments straight up. It looks like the men are in danger of getting "mudded" to death.'

But even the wet and mud could maim. As Private Gardner told a *Yank* reporter that week, 'They pulled us out of the line and when I got out of my hole and started walking I couldn't feel my feet. So I just sat down the first chance I got and took off my shoes. It was the first time I took off my shoes for two weeks and my feet looked bruised and frozen.' But Gardner was too exhausted to bother about them. He fell asleep. Next morning 'my feet were like balloons, so red and swollen I couldn't get my shoes on. And when I tried to walk it was like somebody was sticking needles in my feet.'

Gardner was sent to hospital with trenchfoot, where he remained for 90 days. 'But some guys were a lot worse. Some had big black blisters and a couple had their feet cut off. The doc says you get that from not changing your socks when your feet are wet. Christ, what the hell you

127

gonna do when you're living in a hole for two weeks and the water's up to here and Jerries are shooting at you so you can't go no place.'

But Patton's Third Army *was* going some place. It looked now as if he might breach the Siegfried Line and race for the Rhine before it was too late.

6

THE FORGOTTEN ARMY

On that same 11 November when the young lieutenant blew his top at seeing the bodies of his dead comrades stacked up like logs outside the battalion aid post Patton, at his headquarters in Nancy, was feeling quite pleased. It was his 59th birthday and his fighting divisions were all achieving their objectives despite the terrible conditions under which they were fighting. Soon, he believed, his troops would capture Saarburg and he would be in a position to drive on Trier and from there to the Rhine. It had taken two months longer than he had predicted to get this far, but he was getting there.

At ten past five that November afternoon, when Patton was beginning to fancy his first Bourbon of the day by way of a birthday celebration, Bradley rang up. He congratulated Patton on his birthday and enquired, with apparent casualness, how things were going. In high spirits, Patton told him he would be soon needing Hodges' 83rd Infantry Division to flesh out the coming drive for the Rhine.

Completely out of the blue, Bradley dashed his plans. He said, 'Incidentally Georgie, I don't like the way Walker is planning to handle the 83rd Division. I made it explicitly clear that you can have operational control only to a limited extent. As a matter of fact I don't think you should have the 83rd at all.'

For once Patton was momentarily at a loss for words. Finally he rallied and said, 'But Brad, I need the division! I've made all my plans with them in mind.'

'Walker is disobeying my orders,' Bradley said coldly. 'And I won't let him have the 83rd. No use arguing, George. The decision is final. I'll phone Hodges to this effect.'

The phone went dead. Thus generals played around with the lives of their soldiers, Gods who could decide whether they lived or died on a mere whim or a fit of peevishness.

But such considerations did not come into Pattons' calculations. His concern was that on this, his birthday, Bradley, his one-time subordinate when he had commanded the Seventh Army in Sicily, had virtually ruined his plan to race for the Rhine. As he said bitterly to his staff that night over the celebration dinner, 'Gentlemen, I am sure that this is the first time in the history of war when one-tenth of the attacking general's command was removed after the battle had been joined. Moreover, I am sure that it is a terrible mistake because by using the 83rd we could take Saarburg easily. Without it we won't get Saarburg and will be bothered by the triangle between the Moselle and the Saar.'

Unknown to Hitler, prostrate and sick at his headquarters in the East, Bradley had unwittingly saved his great counter-offensive.

If Patton had received General Macon's 83rd Division and had continued his offensive to the Rhine as planned, the whole left flank of the three assault armies would have been up in the air and Hitler would, in fact, have been unable to launch the attack. As Ladislas Farago, Patton's biographer, has written, 'Patton died convinced that Bradley's decision to take the division from him when he needed it most was one of the great mistakes of the war – probably the decisive factor in making possible, and indeed inevitable, what became the Battle of the Bulge.'

So that night Patton consoled himself by having more than his usual number of 'Armored Diesels', a very potent cocktail invented by his Chief-of-Intelligence, Colonel Koch, and the dire warning that 'The First Army is making a terrible mistake by leaving Middleton's VIII Corps [to which the 83rd Division belonged] static where it is. It is highly probable that the Germans are building up east of them for a terrific blow.'

It was the first warning of what was to come.

★   ★   ★

General Patch was still mourning the loss of his son who had been killed by a direct hit from a German shell. But, as he wrote to his wife on the 14th, 'My hardest period is over. It was during the period after Mac's death when I kept getting letters from you. . . . Always you would tell me in those letters to please not let him get back to his outfit too soon. And I could hardly stand it, knowing I had just done that. I shall never quite be able to forgive myself for that.'

With that off his chest, General Patch wrote of the terrible weather that was hindering his new offensive out of the Vosges: 'For the past week and a half it has been either snowing or raining. . . . It's tough on our men, but equally tough on those Dutch brutes [the Germans who had killed his son].'

But, unknown to the General, the Germans were now pulling back under pressure from his Seventh and de Lattre de Tassigny's First French Armies.

On the Sixth Army Group's left flank, Haislip's 2nd Armoured Division, commanded by General Leclerc, along with the newly arrived 44th Infantry and the veteran 79th Infantry Divisions, were heading for the Saverne Gap. This led out of the Vosges on to the Rhine plain and the glittering prize of Strasbourg beyond. On the right flank de Lattre's men were heading for the Belfort Gap and the Rhine in the region of Mulhouse.

The German commanders defending the Vosges saw the writing on the wall. General Balck's brief was to hold back the Americans until Hitler was ready to attack in the Ardennes. All the same he could not risk two of his armies, the 1st and the 19th, being cut off if the enemy forced the Saverne and Belfort gaps to north and south of them. Leaving behind second-rate troops to hamper the advancing Americans and French as best they could, he ordered his army commanders to make a fighting withdrawal, keeping their forces intact for the Battle of the Rhine to come.

Balck, who was one of the two men at Army Group G privy to the secret of the *Wacht am Rhein** operation, knew what would happen to Hitler's plans if the enemy turned the German right flank. There would be *no* counter-attack.

Now, unknown to Patch, he and his 'Forgotten Army' were going to be given the chance to do something which the flamboyant Patton had failed to realize: to prevent a battle which would become America's Gettysburg of the 20th Century – the Battle of the Bulge. But before that another Allied general would beat him to the Rhine.

★   ★   ★

'King Jean', as his troops called de Lattre de Tassigny, the 1st French Army Commander, was now 54 and at the height of his career. He had command of an army. In two years he had risen from divisional commander to the command of the 1st French Army and he made the

---

* The code name for the coming counter-offensive.

most of it. He loved glittering uniforms, decorations, parades and good living. Champagne was always served at his headquarters. He treated his men like servants and thought nothing of making them wait for hours for his appearance on the parade ground. If he wanted something in the night he wouldn't hesitate to ring for his orderly although what he wanted might well be on his bedside table.

In 1940 he had been chief-of-staff to de Gaulle, but, unlike him, had not gone into exile. Instead he served Pétain as a divisional commander. But when the Germans marched into Unoccupied France in November, 1942, he was the only senior French Army officer to offer them resistance. He was arrested, but escaped to England by submarine.

Now, after months of fighting all the way from the Riviera, his army, a colonial one with many black and brown troops in its ranks, had become demoralized. As de Lattre wrote to de Gaulle in Paris that winter, 'Among all ranks, but particularly among the officers, even at a high level, there is a general impression that the nation is ignoring them and deserting them. The basic cause of this malaise rests in the apparent non-participation of the country in the war.'

De Lattre was right. The French wanted to get on with their lives just as they had done during the *drôle de guerre* period. Most of them had lived a fairly good life until the Allied invasion, especially those who lived on the land. All that Paris saw of the war was the US black market between the Opera and the Madeleine and the drunken GIs in 'Pig Alley'. In the eyes of most French civilians the First Army was wasting its time in some obscure frontier province which was more German than French. It was the Americans who were doing the real fighting.

But now de Lattre saw the opportunity of putting his First Army on the map. His well-rested 1st Corps, preparing to operate out of the Belfort Gap towards the Rhine, had made a spectacular find which would ease their passage considerably. On 14 November de Lattre's 9th Colonial Division prepared to attack. While they waited, an unsuspecting General Friedrich-August Schack, the newly appointed commander of the German 63rd Corps, decided to inspect his positions. He drove to an observation post close to the French, picking up General Hans Oschmann, the head of the 338th Infantry Division, on the way.

Suddenly the 1st French Corps' artillery broke into life. The two generals and their aides ran from their cars into the forest as the French gunners began to pound the area.

When it was over, the Colonial Division started to advance and the generals realized that they were at the point of an enemy attack. Drawing their pistols and followed by their aides, carrying their briefcases, they began to make their way through the forest. But luck was not on their side. Dark shapes, wearing English-type helmets, loomed out of the smoke of war. Oschmann fired, the Moroccans shot back and he fell, mortally wounded. Schack began to run. Behind him the two aides, still with their briefcases, raised their hands in surrender.

French Intelligence chortled when the contents of those briefcases were spread before them at 1st Corps HQ. Not only did they contain a detailed map of the dead General's divisional positions, but they also showed that Oschmann was not prepared in any way for a French attack. The First French Corps had done nothing for so long that the Germans believed they were preparing to dig in for the winter!

So the French went into the attack with even greater élan, knowing that the opposing corps was without its divisional and corps commanders. In addition, that initial barrage had destroyed the German communications network so it was not possible for the German staff to discover what was going on at the front, with the result that the Moroccans made an amazing penetration of six miles. Instantly de Lattre alerted his armour, the 1st Armoured Division, to exploit the penetration.

Despite the bad weather and German road blocks, it began to move for the Rhine. But no alarm bells seemed to sound at Balck's Army Group G.

The next day the French First Armored Division made an advance of three miles, followed by the two supporting colonial infantry divisions, and the extreme right of the First Corps reached the Swiss frontier. Those Germans who could fled across the border and gave themselves up to the Swiss guards. For them the war was over.

On 16 November General Wiese's 338th Infantry Division, facing the French, was so disorganized that the commander of the 19th German Army lost all control over it. That evening Balck signalled Wiese that he had permission to make yet another fighting withdrawal. But Wiese had already done so.

The next day the Germans really started to fall apart. The French, scenting victory, pushed even harder. On the 18th the Germans were in full retreat, with the survivors of the shattered 338th Infantry Division escaping the advancing French the best they could in small leaderless groups.

In vain the divisional command set up roadblocks and stop lines, manned by heavily armed officers and military policemen. But as soon as they had reorganized a group into some semblance of a fighting formation, it would slip away into the forest.

French losses were mounting, but de Lattre brooked no slowing down of his drive. He wanted the kudos of being the first Allied general to reach the Rhine. He would show the Americans that his ragtag army with its obsolete weapons and battered equipment was better than theirs.

On the afternoon of the 19th an advance detachment of his First Armoured Division sneaked through a German position. The platoon of medium tanks and one of armoured infantry under the command of Lieutenant Jean Carrelet de Loisy of the 2nd African Chasseurs scuttled across the snowbound plain heading for the river. When they saw it de Loisy's face broke into a smile. They had done it! An hour later the little group, spread out in a defensive perimeter, was joined by the 2nd Battalion of the 68th African Artillery. The African artillery loaded their guns and lobbed a few shells across the water. They were the first French shells to land on German soil since the débâcle of May, 1940. The breakthrough had been achieved.*

*　*　*

'*Mon General*, here I can do no more. I ask your permission to take my chance.' *Capitaine le Vicomte* de Hautecloque was asking his divisional commander for permission to desert.

On this twenty-eighth day of May, 1940, with the heavy guns of the permanent barrage rumbling in the distance and the long pathetic columns of refugees heading south fleeing before the ever-victorious German Army, the 37-year-old Captain knew that the French Army was beaten. Soon it would lay down its arms to the Germans. Not he! The scion of the de Hautecloques would continue to fight the *Boche* wherever he could.

Thus Leclerc, as he would be soon known, left his own beaten division and attempted to join the five French divisions reported still fighting around Lille. But by the time he reached them the fighting was over and what was left of those five divisions were on the run.

So Leclerc found himself a fugitive in his own country. Not only was he on the run from the Germans, but his countrymen seemed to have no time for him either. More than once he was refused food by his fellow citizens. Once even a priest turned him away in case the Germans shot him for harbouring a fugitive French officer. Leclerc seemed to be the

---

* De Loisy was killed in action at Mulhouse five days later.

only man left in France who still wanted to fight the Germans. At one stage on his flight south he was captured, but managed to talk his way out. On another occasion he was wounded in a dive-bombing attack by Stukas and awoke to find himself in a hospital recently captured by the *Boche*. Again he escaped.

Shortly after that second escape he was one of the few Frenchmen who bothered to listen to a broadcast from London, given by a penniless fugitive from France who would soon be condemned to death in his absence by the godfather of his own child.* On that memorable 17 June, 1940, the voice from London thundered: 'France is not alone. I, General de Gaulle, now in London, call on all officers and soldiers in Britain or who come to Britain, with or without arms, to join me. . . . Whatever happens, the flame of French resistance must not and will not go out.'

In the event only 7,000 out of the 90,000 French troops in Britain elected to join de Gaulle, but the fugitive was stirred by that impassioned appeal. He knew what to do. Six weeks later, now bearing the name of Leclerc to protect his wife and five children from any possible reprisals, he was on his way to French Africa to rally the French colonies there to de Gaulle. 'Your immediate objective,' de Gaulle had told him at their first meeting in London, 'is to rally French Africa. Your long term policy is to free France.'

A year later Leclerc, helped by the British,** had marched across Africa at the head of a motley army of white colonial and native troops. He had come 3,000 miles through the jungle, over mountains and across the desert to attack an Italian fort which controlled the oasis of Kufra in the Sahara.

For five days Leclerc's men fought the numerically superior Italians. Then, when his guns were virtually out of ammunition, Leclerc saw a white flag flying over the Beau Geste-like fort. The Italians had surrendered. He at once signalled to de Gaulle that the Free French flag flew again above Kufra. It was De Gaulle's first victory. Leclerc ended his cable with the proud boast: 'We will not rest until the flag of France also flies over Paris and Strasbourg.'

This declaration, which French military historians call the 'Oath of

---

* Marshal Pétain, the head of the new Vichy Government in Unoccupied France was the godfather of one of de Gaulle's two children.
** After the war de Gaulle made no mention in his books of the British role in the reviving of *la Gloire*. In all the missions carried out in Africa the British played a vital part. Even the great march across Africa was carried out with officers of the British Long Range Desert Group at the head of the column, navigating from start to finish.

Kufra' would become part of the legend of a renewed and revitalized France. Four years later Leclerc's Second French Armoured Division was allowed to capture Paris, courtesy of Patton's Third Army. The first part of the Oath of Kufra had been fulfilled. Thereafter there had been trouble. Leclerc was ordered to take his division and join de Lattre's 1st French Army coming up from the south of France.

Leclerc refused, saying that he would rather disband his division. He added, 'I will not serve with any commander who previously obeyed Vichy and whom I consider to be turncoats.' The Americans tried to reason with him, but Leclerc wouldn't budge. As General Patch said of him when he joined the Seventh Army, Leclerc made it 'distinctly clear' that he 'did not want to serve with the First French Army'. This was the first time that Patch and his boss, Devers, had had trouble with their French subordinates, but it was not to be the last.★

The Americans could understand Leclerc's reluctance to serve under de Lattre. General Marshall, the head of the US Army, called de Lattre a 'politico who never achieved any of his objectives on time'. General Bradley referred to him as a 'skunk at a kitten party'. So in the end Leclerc was left with Haislip's XV Corps, now part of Patch's Seventh. In the plump American Leclerc found a sympathetic chief. Haislip had been a student at the *Ecole de Guerre*, spoke fluent French and was by nature a francophile. 'I never issued orders to Leclerc,' he said after the war. 'Whenever I wanted him to do something, I would say, "Leclerc, this is what I am planning to do. It looks to me as though you could do this and that and so forth. I want you to go away and study it and tell me what you think".'

Now, in the third week of September, Leclerc's 2nd Armored Division was officially in reserve, while the American 79th and 44th Divisions slogged away getting through the Saverne Gap. But Leclerc was already poring over his maps of Alsace. As one aide recalled later, 'He searched for little entries, little narrow roads, or even tracks through which he might infiltrate his tanks. It was the same as he had done at Kufra.'

The aide was correct. General Leclerc was determined to fulfil the second promise he had made at Kufra. Now he would liberate Strasbourg.

★ After the war Montgomery also had trouble with de Lattre. Talking to King George VI, he said, 'De Lattre is quite unsound', adding, 'I think I can sum up, sir, by describing him as the French equivalent of Dickie Mountbatten.'

7

THE RACE FOR STRASBOURG

It was Thanksgiving Day, 1944, when General Haislip's XV Corps began its move out of the Saverne Gap, heading for the plain below and the Rhine. It was a wild night with the rain slanting down in the beams cast by their headlights. For although the US Army always drove blacked-out, Leclerc, the commander of Haislip's armoured division, had ordered his drivers to keep their headlights on. It was the only way for his convoys to get through narrow winding roads of the Vosges, selected personally by him, and surprise the *Boche* dug in on the plain below.

There were a few Americans with Leclerc's division. Lieutenant Tony Triumpho of the attached US artillery battalion was one of them. It was his task to set up a forward observation post for Leclerc, who liked to direct his own artillery fire from the front: 'The plan was for the French to get just over the other side of the Vosges and then wait for the American infantry to come up for a combined attack on Strasbourg.' But, as Triumpho admitted after the war, 'The French, of course, had another plan.'

As the two armoured columns moved forward on two separate routes the atmosphere in the commandeered château in the wooded foothills of the Vosges which was Leclerc's HQ was tense. Captain Chatel, who had joined the Second Armoured Division from the Resistance, tried to snatch some sleep on the floor, but Leclerc 'kept coming in and asking whether there was any news of the drive.' Leclerc was restless. It was not just that he wanted to cross the Vosges that stormy night. He wanted more. He wanted Strasbourg.

The first news to come in was good. One of his officers who had served with him in Africa, a Major Massu,* had reached the little town

* Later the parachute commander General Massu who rebelled against de Gaulle in North Africa in 1958.

of Dabo *on the other side of the Vosges*. After a hard slog of two months a unit of Patch's Seventh Army had finally crossed the mountain range.

Leclerc leapt into action. He ordered Captain Chatel to drive to General Haislip's HQ immediately. 'Tell him' he said, 'that I need one or two battalions of American infantry to clean up the roads behind us and deal with all the prisoners. We don't want to be bothered waiting about to take prisoners. Bring me those battalions yourself, Captain.'

Off went Chatel into the wild night. How was a humble captain to persuade a corps commander to give him two infantry battalions?

Haislip was asleep when Chatel arrived at his headquarters at Luneville, but somehow Chatel got the duty officer to wake the Corps Commander and, as Chatel recalled afterwards, 'He was very nice about it'. Chatel put forward Leclerc's request. Initially Haislip refused, 'because armor has a bad habit of trying to borrow soldiers from infantry divisions to save getting their own infantry chewed up,' which was in fact Leclerc's intention. He was saving his own armoured infantry for the street fighting to come. But in the end Haislip gave in. The French could have two battalions from the 'Cross of Lorraine', the 79th Infantry Division.

Chatel was about to rush away with the good news when the phone rang. It was Patch. To Chatel, who understood English, it was clear that Patch was forbidding any drive on Strasbourg by the French 2nd Armored Division. Then he heard Haislip say, 'Sir, we cannot take "no" completely for an answer. Will you please confirm that it can be done?'

An argument between the two generals followed. 'I heard General Haislip argue,' Chatel recalled afterwards, 'that Strasbourg was important not only strategically but because of the oath Leclerc had taken at Kufra. In the end General Patch said Leclerc could send out a patrol in that direction [Strasbourg] but it was not to start running before General Haislip gave the order.'

Then Haislip turned to Chatel and said, 'You can do it, but only on my order. General Leclerc knows of course, that he is only supposed to take the passes of the Vosges and not to go further.' If he did, Haislip reminded Chatel, he would be driving into the operational zone of the Seventh Army's 6th Corps. Chatel said he realized that. Then he was gone. 'When I got back,' he said, 'three of the five gaps [in the Vosges] had been crossed and our forward tanks were in a position to push on.'

He gave Leclerc his good news, had a quick cup of coffee and was soon on his way back to Haislip's HQ with a new message. Progress was good and the 2nd Armored Division might now be in a position to send patrols in the direction of Strasbourg if the Corps Commander gave his permission.

Chatel arrived at Haislips's HQ before the morning briefing. There he bumped into an old friend on the Corps Commander's staff who said, 'Ah, Chatel, next time we see you, maybe we'll have a drink at Hotel Metropole in Strasbourg.'

At that moment Haislip himself came into the room and overheard the remark. He said in a loud voice so that everyone could hear, 'This is a joke of course. You know that you can't go to Strasbourg.'

Chatel related his message and asked, 'Will you confirm, sir, that we can now send a patrol in that direction?'

Haislip nodded and Chatel was off like a shot. Back at Leclerc's HQ he gave the General the news he wanted. Thereupon Leclerc gave the orders for 'a patrol' to advance on Strasbourg.

In fact Haislip knew full well what Leclerc was up to, although his drive on Strasbourg ran contrary not only to Devers' but also to Eisenhower's orders. After the war the Corps Commander stated, 'I told Leclerc, "This is your country. Strasbourg is yours. You can capture it and I will not even go into the town. We won't claim it as an American victory. It shall be entirely a French victory – *your victory!*"'

Now the 'patrol' became a full-scale attack on Strasbourg. Phalsbourg was taken, the Germans being caught completely off guard. The commanding general there went into the bag with hundreds of other Germans. Outside the town the French halted and set up an ambush. They had learnt from prisoners that the Germans were still sending reinforcements through Phalsbourg. So the German convoy rolled right into the trap, the Germans not even aware that the French had come out of the mountains.

One of the ambushers, Emil Frey, a volunteer who came from London and was half-English, remembered, 'It was an absolute massacre. We just let them come as close as possible and then shot them to bits. They were all sorts, lorried infantry, guns, staff cars and even the German Chief of Railways for the region. We poured fire into them until the roads were absolutely littered with burning vehicles.'

The French pressed on. Watching them move out BBC war correspondent Wynford Vaughan-Thomas recorded, 'The drivers drive with bare hands. Their gloves can't grip the slippery wheels that whirl this way and that and move with every bump and pothole and everything slithering on the road. On they go, these endless, urgent columns, crowding every highway, debouching into the rough country tracks that are seething glaciers of mud.'

Sergeant Bill Maudlin, formerly of the Seventh Army's 45th Division and now a cartoonist with the *Stars and Stripes*, was so impressed by the way the French drove that he drew a cartoon on the subject for the Army newspaper. It showed a long row of US Army Truck drivers being addressed by their lieutenant before departure on convoy work. 'Men,' says the young officer very gravely, 'some of you may never come back. *There's a French convoy on the road today!*'

What impact the French drivers had on their American counterparts is not known. What is known, however, is that the French slaughtered hundreds of Germans, and Frenchmen, on the road to Strasbourg. Nothing seemed able to stop them. But now General Eisenhower decided to take a hand in the game.

★   ★   ★

On the morning of the ambush an American colonel appeared in the 2nd Armored Division area asking if he could speak to General Leclerc. The staff guessed at once that here was a messenger sent to stop the drive on Strasbourg. Colonel Girard, who was there, remembers that 'a friend of mine, who was very quick-witted, said, "I know where he is. I'll take you to him straight away." He then took the American off in the opposite direction. When Leclerc was not to be found, he said the General must have moved somewhere else and so he took the colonel off to another place.' In the end the American gave up.

Now the staff posted officers at key crossroads in order to delay any attempt by the Supreme Commander to stop their drive on Strasbourg. Captain Chatel recalls how he was told to 'take General Monoher, Chief-of-Staff to General Haislip, to tell General Leclerc *not* to attack Strasbourg. Apparently General Haislip had received a direct order from General Eisenhower that we were not to attempt to take Strasbourg. Eisenhower had been informed that we were already moving right out of our zone of operations and he had ordered us to stop.'

Again they gave the staff officer the run-around, taking him along roads that were blocked or where the bridges had been blown so that the car could go no further. In the end General Monoher tumbled to the fact that he was being tricked. He demanded to know where Leclerc was. The French officers said they had no idea, so General Monoher said he'd go and find him by himself. By the time he did it would be all over.

★   ★   ★

At dawn on the morning of 23 November Leclerc gave the order to take Strasbourg by a surprise attack. The Germans had a garrison of 15,000 soldiers in the city and Leclerc knew that, in addition to the several thousand Germans who lived there, a sizeable proportion of the Alsatians were pro-German. In order to capture the city he would have to catch the German garrison off guard. He wanted no Alsatian betraying his attack to the enemy.

Triumpho was one of the three-man American jeep team at the point that day. 'We went roaring across the plain in our jeep,' he recalled afterwards, 'along with four or five light tanks and a few halftracks of infantry. We passed working parties and groups of German troops and they just stood open-mouthed. When they saw we were French troops they were scared to death, for they had heard that the French did not take too many prisoners.'

But the French were too intent on capturing Strasbourg to waste time shooting prisoners. Every minute counted. The Frenchmen strained their eyes to catch the first glimpse of Strasbourg's famous cathedral. Then, there it was. They had reached the city which Leclerc had sworn to capture all those years before. He had almost fulfilled the Oath of Kufra.

At his temporary HQ Leclerc discovered that the telephone lines to Strasbourg were still intact. He put an officer who spoke fluent German on the line and the latter cried over the phone, as if he were in extreme difficulty, 'We need help here urgently! Send up a battalion!'

Up came the German infantry battalion at the double and went straight into the bag. The defenders were now minus one battalion and, as General Haislip remarked after the war, long after Leclerc was dead, 'Leclerc told me about it with the greatest glee. He simply loved that sort of stuff.'

Dennis Woodcock, a Quaker driving an ambulance with the French, although he was an Englishman, remembers how it was as they entered Strasbourg. 'The Germans hadn't the faintest idea of what was happening and went straight into the trap. When we burst into Strasbourg, the Germans were absolutely flabbergasted. Thousands were not fighting men at all. They were civilians, administrative people, going around carrying briefcases, shopping or out with their wives. We landed right in the middle of them and the battle-stained French soldiers looked quite out of place.'

Now, as fierce fire fights broke out all over the city, the French rushed the German barracks, filled with replacements for the front. They were not even armed and went behind the wire in their hundreds, then in their thousands. They were packed into the city's main squares, each square holding up to two or three thousand prisoners.

But, although there were plenty of German troops holding out in Strasbourg, the code message 'cloth in iodine' was flashed back to Leclerc's command post. It meant that Strasbourg was taken.

Devers, who happened to be up front that day watching the Seventh Army, had no idea what was going on. He thought that the French 2nd Armored Division was still in reserve. Haislip then surprised the Army Group Commander with the news that Leclerc's armour was running wild in the city.

Now Leclerc himself arrived. Behind him in the second vehicle was Captain Chatel. He was amazed by what he saw that November day. 'There were some fantastic things happening. As we passed a barber's I saw a German officer shot as he was coming out to a staff car waiting at the kerb. The street cars were still running and many of the Germans, mainly non-combat troops, were going about their duties quite oblivious of us. Then I saw the most moving thing. As the townspeople realized that we were French many of them fell to their knees, crying with joy and uttering prayers of thanksgiving. We drove straight for the Kaiserpalast, where the German High Command and Gestapo HQ were. When we arrived cups of coffee poured out for the German staff, now under guard, were still hot. That is how great the surprise was!'

★　　★　　★

Now they came to the Rhine and Tony Triumpho decided to have a go. With the other two of his jeep team, 'we raced right across Strasbourg and crossed the Rhine to Kehl on the German side,' he recalled later. 'There seemed nobody about. We made a reconnaissance to find out what we could and all we heard was the chirping of the birds. It was most eerie and deserted.' They raced back to France unharmed.

Not far away the BBC war correspondent recorded for his listeners back home, 'There it is, set against the rain-dark sky to the east, a looming outline of distant hills – the Black Forest, the western barrier to Hitler's Reich. We felt we'd come to an end of a long journey. *We'd got to the Rhine at last!*'

That afternoon General de Gaulle told the French Assembly that Strasbourg was French once more. Not far away the Supreme

Commander, in his headquarters at Versailles, did not rejoice at the news. Nor was he cheered by the fact that already Leclerc was posting notices throughout the city to the effect that he would have sharpshooters and those who sheltered them 'summarily shot without trial'. Already there had been cases of newly appointed French officials being assassinated by pro-German Alsatians. He also proclaimed that he would have five German hostages shot for every one of his own men murdered by snipers.

Something had to be done. General Devers was told that orders like this contravened international law. Besides it would not look good in US newspapers if Frenchmen were shooting Frenchmen out of hand. But the problem escalated. It was reliably reported that General 'Iron Mike' O'Daniel, the commander of the 3rd Infantry Division, which had just sent a regiment to help the French in Strasbourg, supported the move. The General maintained that no one was going to shoot the soldiers of his division and get away with it. 'Shoot 'em and be damned,' he said. He was ordered to retract the statement, which, in the end, he did.

Leclerc was made of harder stuff. When the French Military Governor of Strasbourg was commanded by Devers to put up posters stating that the Sixth Army Group had always conformed to the Geneva Convention, Leclerc advised him not to obey. He didn't.

Leclerc was grateful to the Americans, especially Wade Haislip. But still he felt that they didn't understand France's problems. De Gaulle's government was very shaky. The communists, the most powerful political party in the land, were making problems. Throughout France de Gaulle's men were paying off old scores. Those who had worked with the Germans or had supported Vichy were being brought to trial. Justice was summary and it was estimated many years later that some 100,000 French men and women were sentenced to death that winter. As Leclerc saw it, this was no time to go soft on those who sabotaged, sniped at or didn't support the new masters of Strasbourg. Indeed when a few days later de Gaulle made an appearance in Strasbourg to attend a thanksgiving Mass, the men of the 2nd Armored were forced to give up their blankets, despite the bitter weather, to cover the windows of the cathedral so that he was protected from snipers' bullets and shrapnel. Desperate times, in Leclerc's opinion, demanded desperate measures.

Eisenhower was incensed. Not only didn't he like Leclerc's unauthorized seizure of Strasbourg, but he was highly displeased by the manner in which he was governing the city. He even ordered Leclerc to have the original German Street signs restored to avoid 'administrative chaos', though he did stop short of having the 'Adolf Hitler Platz' returned.

It was time, Eisenhower concluded, that he had a closer look at General Devers' Sixth Army Group. Devers had to be told to obey his orders – or else.

8

THE BIG DECISION

As Eisenhower travelled eastwards, driven by his chauffeur-cum-mistress Kay Summersby, who, although she was British, now sported her bars as a second lieutenant in the American WAC, he was not in a particularly good mood. The weather was terrible; he had been receiving a lot of nagging letters from his wife and he didn't like what Devers was doing with his Sixth Army Group.

His mood wasn't helped by the knowledge that Montgomery had flown to London to discuss with Alan Brooke some means of dealing with Eisenhower and 'counter the pernicious American strategy of attacking all along the line'. He knew that Montgomery had proposed a change in the whole command set-up. The plan was for Bradley to take over control of all the ground forces, with Montgomery commanding all Allied forces north of the Ardennes and Devers all those to the south. In essence, what all this meant was that the British did not have any faith in his competence as commander of the ground forces, a post he had taken over at General Marshall's instigation in September.

On 24 November Eisenhower stopped first at Patton's HQ in Nancy. What he learned there didn't help his mood either. Patton was attacking along water-logged roads. His armour, which used the fields, was bogging down and the Third Army was experiencing difficulty in bringing up the supplies that Patton was always screaming for. Morale was low in the Third Army with a high rate of non-battle casualties, due to trenchfoot, chest disease and the usual number of self-inflicted wounds. (Patton had just ordered that anyone with a wounded hand or foot should be carefully examined by the medics for powder burns, indicating that it was a self-inflicted wound. To get round that, his men started shooting at their hands and feet through a loaf of bread, which prevented powder burns). In Patton's view his failure to make progress in Lorraine was due to the failings of Hodges, Montgomery and Devers. In reality what was stopping him advancing was simply the obstinate German *Landser*!

During their short stopover in Nancy Patton urged Eisenhower and Bradley, who had journeyed down from his HQ in Luxembourg, either to give part of his seventy-mile front to Devers or return Haislip's XV Corps to him. Patton preferred the latter and Bradley supported his Third Army Commander. Bradley didn't like Devers. He had served under him for a few days in London where 'I studied Devers closely,' as he wrote after the war, 'and formed my own independent opinion of the man. I found him overly garrulous, saying little of importance, egotistical, intolerant, not very smart and much too inclined to rush off half-cocked.' It was a damning indictment of a fellow American general, but one, however, which Eisenhower shared, as his post-war assessment of Devers shows. Eisenhower called him 'a .22 calibre general', not a very flattering description of a lieutenant-general commanding an army group. So they left Patton's HQ with their minds presumably made up about what they should allow Devers to do now he had reached the Rhine. Patton was going to make the running. They drove on south, their Packard flanked by flashily dressed outriders, Eisenhower cradling his and Kay's funny little 'Scotty' in his arms, his mood foul.

That Friday morning they were met with a surprise as the car drove into the courtyard of Haislip's HQ. The Corps Commander ran out to meet them shouting at Eisenhower, 'For God's sake, sir, I was just on my way down to tell you not to come. Please go on. We don't want you.'

Eisenhower looked startled and Haislip explained, 'There is a report of an armoured breakthrough on the front held by our cavalry.' The drivers of Eisenhower's convoy noted that Haislip's staff were preparing for a fight and they reckoned that when headquarters staff had to fight it was time for generals to get out.

But Eisenhower was not having it. He laughed and said to Haislip, 'Dammit, Ham, you invited me to lunch and I'm not going to leave until I get it.'

But Eisenhower's relaxed mood didn't last long when he discovered that Haislip's staff, despite the sudden emergency, were making plans to cross the Rhine. From there the little convoy drove to Brooks' 6th Corps HQ. The normally serious Brooks was relaxed and obviously very pleased with himself. He had finally brought his corps down out of the Vosges, a tricky operation which no general had managed before. Now he, too, was planning a crossing of the Rhine as soon as possible. Without any consultation with Eisenhower's headquarters in Versailles, his staff, just like that of Haislip's XV Corps, were busy drawing up plans for an assault crossing of the Rhine! In the area between Strasbourg and the German city of Rastatt, they intended to build up initial bridgeheads on German soil to be exploited as soon as they got the green light.

This information made Eisenhower very angry and he ordered the two corps commanders to stop planning for a Rhine crossing at once. At Haislip's HQ Eisenhower even issued *verbal* orders to halt all preparations for a Rhine crossing, changing the direction of the corps' advance immediately to head northwards in support of Patton's Third Army. Supporting Patton's advance into the Saar Basin was to be given first priority.

Devers couldn't believe his ears. After nearly three months of attacking the Siegfried Line, Bradley's 12th Army Group had merely forced a gap between Geilenkirchen and Aachen. It was of little use, for the Germans had concentrated the bulk of their reserves there to prevent a breakthrough to Cologne on the Rhine some fifty miles away. Now here he was already on the Rhine, separated from Germany by perhaps a hundred yards of water. Already some patrols from the Third Division had been across and had encountered little in the way of resistance on the German side. Why was Eisenhower now asking him to be little more than a flank guard to Patton, when the glittering prize of a Rhine crossing was within his grasp?

Devers knew that Eisenhower disliked him. He was the only general Eisenhower had not selected; all the others had been vetted by him personally. Marshall, who thought highly of him, had appointed Devers to his command and Devers knew that it was common gossip at the Supreme Commander's Versailles HQ that Eisenhower only retained him because he hated busting lieutenant generals.

Returning to his own headquarters, temporarily stunned by the way 'Ike' had reacted, Devers determined to fight back. For a good while he marshalled his thoughts at the Hotel Hermitage at Vittel where his HQ was. He knew that Eisenhower and Bradley would be coming across later for a formal dinner. He wanted to be prepared for them. For nearly two years now, ever since he had arrived in the ETO, Ike had been bugging him. Now he was going to fight back. Always the Supreme Commander had favoured Bradley and Patton, who always grabbed the headlines. The time had come for the Seventh to grab some of those headlines. That was the way the war was fought by the US Army in the winter of 1944.

★ ★ ★

That Saturday, as Devers prepared to have it out with Eisenhower and Bradley and the *Stars and Stripes* reported triumphantly that Strasbourg had been captured and that the first 'reconnaissance patrols' of the Seventh Army had crossed the Rhine, Leclerc was summoned to Haislip's XV Corps HQ. On the morrow he had planned a victory parade on the Place Kléber at which he would inform the world that Strasbourg was French again. Now the francophile Corps Commander told his subordinate that Eisenhower wasn't happy with Leclerc's capture of the Alsatian city and that Eisenhower, as well as De Gaulle, had suggested that Leclerc and his 2nd Armored Division should join de Lattre's 1st French Army to clean up what was left of General Wiese's German 19th Army around Colmar.

Leclerc, who wanted to gain the kudos of being the first French general to cross the Rhine with the US Seventh Army, would have nothing of it. He told Haislip, 'I want you to tell General Devers something from me. It is that I, myself, and every man in my division are volunteers. We do not have to fight and we do not want to fight, but we do for the liberation and honour of France. But if we are ever attached to the divisions of de Lattre de Tassigny, we will pack up and go home.'

Haislip was shocked, but he could see just how serious the French general was. As he reported later to Devers, who 'was storming around a bit' at the news, 'I can promise you, Leclerc is going to do this. For I know the fellow thoroughly. Whether it sounds reasonable or unreasonable, he's not going to serve under de Lattre.'

As one of his soldiers, Gaston Eve, recalled years later, 'Leclerc saw in his division a perfect blend, a homogeneous collection of men representative of all that was good and bad in France. The *2ᵉ Division Blindée* was the new France. And now he was concerned and alarmed that if it came under the command of the French First Army it would be corrupted and spoiled. Leclerc didn't want to keep away from de Lattre's command through any petty professional jealousy. It was because he feared that the "bad old France", still obviously prevalent in de Lattre's army, the emphasis on pleasing Paris and the politicians, might tarnish the valiant and shining spirit of the splendid new France in his division.'

In the end, in order to please Haislip, whom Leclerc regarded as somewhat of a father figure, he agreed to go – temporarily. But it wouldn't be long before he was back with Patch's Seventh Army. Indeed he would end the war racing the US 3rd and 101st Airborne Divisions for the honour of capturing Hitler's home in the mountains beyond Berchtesgaden.*

★　　★　　★

Thus, while Haislip tried to reason with the prickly French general, Devers prepared to do battle with Eisenhower and Bradley. The three commanders had a late dinner in the Hotel Hermitage in Vittel and then retired to Devers' private office to discuss the matter of the Rhine crossings.

Eisenhower opened the meeting by stating that, before any crossing of the Rhine should be undertaken, all the remaining troops of General Wiese's 19th German Army should be cleared from the west bank. Devers, according to Eisenhower, retorted that the French 1st Army 'could easily take care of them', as 'the German Nineteenth had ceased to exist as a tactical force'.

Eisenhower thought that 'Devers' estimate of the French First Army's immediate effectiveness was 'overoptimistic' and that he 'probably underrated the defensive power of German units when they set themselves stubbornly to hold a strong position'.

The discussion grew more heated. Eisenhower continued to insist that the Sixth Army Group Commander should forget his proposed Rhine crossing. Instead he should turn his Seventh Army north immediately to assist Patton in the Saar. This went against his current SHAEF directive which provided for any opportunistic crossing of the Rhine by any commander during the November offensive.

Now Eisenhower put on the pressure. He suggested that he might take two divisions away from the Seventh and that Haislip's Corps might well have to take on a larger area of territory to the north-west, thus weakening its effectiveness. Devers objected. He said it was Patch's Seventh Army that should be reinforced, not Patton's, bogged down in the mud of Lorraine. Here Bradley stepped in. He said that any attempt to force the Rhine and the West Wall defences beyond would be foolhardy. Devers surprised him by answering that he already had several patrols

---

* Before that happened, however, Leclerc received a letter from the French Supreme Court stating that the death sentence placed upon him by the Vichy Régime had been rescinded. It seemed to him typical of the bad old France that the notification had to be sent to him 'through channels'. A year later he was dead.

across the river and they had found the West Wall defences there completely unmanned.

This left Eisenhower in the cold. With that ear-to-ear smile noticeably absent, he told Devers to use whatever strength he had to clean up the west bank of the Rhine. There would be no Rhine crossing. Then he compromised, stating that, if Devers agreed, he could keep his two divisions. Indeed Devers would be given a second armoured division if he would agree to the Supreme Commander's proposals.

It was blackmail, of course, but Devers had no alternative. By now it was the small hours of the morning and the three men were tired and angry. Eisenhower came out of the meeting 'as mad as hell', while Devers retired to his bedroom wondering, as he recorded in his diary, if he was 'a member of the same team'.

★   ★   ★

Prior to that meeting Devers, Patch and Haislip had been certain that the latter's XV Corps would have no difficulty in seizing a bridgehead between Rastatt and Strasbourg. This bridgehead would have been exploited by Brooks' VI Corps. It would have headed northwards, outflanking the whole of the West Wall along the Rhine. Four months later when the 'most famous bridge in the world', the one at Remagen on the Rhine, was seized, Eisenhower had no hesitation in tossing aside the grand strategic plan which envisaged Montgomery crossing in style in the last week of March, 1945. He immediately reinforced the 9th Armored Division's bridgehead at this most unlikely spot on the Rhine (no road network to speak of, surrounding hilly country) with four divisions. Why was he not prepared to do so now in November, 1944 after Devers had assured him that his assault divisions would meet with little resistance?

We don't know. That meeting, which had a profound effect on the rest of the war in the West, is virtually totally unknown to the student of the Second World War. Eisenhower doesn't mention it directly in his *Crusade in the West*. All he refers to are the orders he gave to Devers. Bradley mentions it not at all in his memoirs. We only know that it took place at all from Devers' personal diary and one kept by one of Bradley's aides, though he gives no details of what transpired. It seems as if Eisenhower and Bradley never wanted the general public to know after the war that the Rhine could have been crossed in 1944.

Three decades after the event General Garrison Davidson, the 7th Army's engineer, who would have been responsible for moving the

Army's two assault divisions across the Rhine, wrote: 'It is interesting to conjecture what might have been the effect of the exploitation of an unexpected crossing of the Rhine in late November. . . . I have often wondered what might have happened if [Eisenhower] had had the audacity to take a calculated risk as General Patton would have, instead of playing it safe. Perhaps success would have eliminated any possibility of the Battle of the Bulge. 40,000 casualties there could have been avoided and the war shortened by a number of months at the saving of thousands of lives.'

★   ★   ★

On the same day that Eisenhower ordered Haislip to stop planning a crossing of the Rhine Hitler issued an order to his top commander who would lead the assault in the Ardennes. It began with words: 'Frederick II earned his title "the Great" not because he was victorious, but because he did not despair in adversity; equally posterity will come to recognize me because I, too, will not have surrendered after grievous misfortune. *The Ardennes will be my Rossbach!'*★

It had been decided that November day that the *Wehrmacht* would launch the great attack in the Ardennes. But the date of the assault had been postponed due to the objections to Hitler's plan by some of his generals and the late arrival of some of the units which would attack. Now some 200,000 assault troops were massed in the hilly forests of the German Eifel opposite the 80,000 GIs of Middleton's 8th Corps. They would attack at 5.50 on the morning of Saturday, 16 December. Eisenhower had exactly twenty-four days left. *Death on a distant frontier had only just begun.*

★ Famous battle won by Frederick the Great at Rossbach against an allied coalition in 1757.

9

ENVOI

'Remember me when I am dead and simplify me when I am dead.'
Keith Douglas, Captain, Royal Armoured Corps
(Killed in action, Normandy, 1944).

On the last day of March, 1945, after the Anglo-Americans had all crossed the Rhine – eight days before Patton had noted in his diary, 'Today I pissed in the Rhine' – Charles de Gaulle wired de Lattre, the commander of the 1st French Army, which had been on the river since 16 November, 1944, 'My dear General, you must cross the Rhine even if the Americans are not agreeable, and even if you have to cross in rowing boats. It is a matter of the greatest national importance. Karlsruhe and Stuttgart await you – even if they do not want you.'

Sensitive as always about his own position and prestige – and naturally *la gloire de la France* – de Gaulle wanted the world to see that he and France were playing a full part in these world-shaking events on his country's frontier. True, he had once said that the Anglo-Saxons should do all the fighting and be killed if necessary. France would need all the soldiers she could muster for the problems of the post-war world. But now de Gaulle was prepared to risk casualties for the sake of the world-wide publicity that would greet a French crossing of the river which France had always maintained was not just a German waterway but her border with France

De Lattre gave the task to General Monsabert, the commander of his 2nd Corps. Monsabert was ordered to cross that night at the German town of Speyer. Two years before the French Corps Commander had loyally supported Vichy. Indeed he had taken part in the fight against the

British and Americans when they landed in North Africa in 1942. But although he was not a follower of de Gaulle, he still understood the importance of a French crossing of the Rhine.

There was, however, a catch. General Patch and his boss, Devers, didn't want the French to cross. The two American generals knew that the French objective was Stuttgart, but that city had been allotted to the Americans in their future zone of occupation in a beaten Germany. So at first they refused Monsabert any boats. In the end they gave way and said they would send up some paddle boats (the Americans had used power boats for the crossing of their Seventh Army).

All that afternoon the men of the French 3me Régiment de Tirailleurs waited impatiently for the promised craft. Finally, after nightfall, an American truck appeared bringing with it – *one single rubber dinghy!*

The French reaction is not recorded. Still honour had to be satisfied. So a certain Sergeant Bertout and ten of his men clambered into the boat and rowed across the Rhine. It is doubtful whether the Germans on the opposite bank realized that they were being invaded by the *Franzmaenner* for the first time since Napoleon. At all events they didn't react until daylight when they started shelling a second crossing near the small German town of Germersheim.

But the crossing turned into a tragedy and the 100-metre-broad 'bridgehead' was held only because the French artillery pounded the Germans all day long to prevent a counter-attack. Eventually the Americans took pity on the French and General Brooks of the Seventh Army's VI Corps agreed to allow twenty French trucks bearing infantry to cross the Rhine using the American bridge at Mannheim. Thus honour was satisfied.

So the wheel turned full circle. The scruffy bunch of one-time collaborators, renegades, *pieds noirs* and North African colonial soldiers had managed to do what Leclerc and his volunteers had failed to do. They were the ones who crossed the Rhine, not Leclerc. Aptly enough the date was 1 April, 1945 – April Fool's Day.

Thousands of Anglo-Saxon soldiers had preceded them, in some cases suffering heavy casualties to get across the river. But only the French erected a monument to celebrate the crossing of Sergeant Bertout and his ten Algerians. It is still there, a stone pillar, the height of a man, bearing the palm twig of the French Army, a carved scimitar and some letters in Arabic. Beneath them, chiselled into the stone, is an inscription which reads:

'Le 31 mars 1945 3° Rgt de Tirailleurs
Algériens franchit de Rhin
L'operation fut executée par le groupe Franc
du Régiment de Ier Battaillon et les Sappeurs
de la 83/1 Cie.

It was to be a lasting tribute to the glory of France – and, naturally, to General Charles de Gaulle too.

★   ★   ★

So the French at last crossed the Rhine which they had first reached five months earlier. A month later the war was over and peace returned to Europe. But on that distant frontier along which the West Wall ran peace didn't come so quickly. For a long time afterwards the French, British, Americans, Belgians and Luxembourgers systematically blew up every remaining bunker and pillbox as if they half-expected a new army of invading Teutons to spring from the war-torn earth. On both sides of the frontier the starving locals risked their lives to forage for the canned food left behind by the departed soldiers.

In the end the engineers departed, but still that distant frontier didn't come to rest. Now local newspapers were calling it the 'sinful frontier', across which bold if crooked men, who weren't afraid to kill if necessary, transported their wares to sell on the black market which thrived in Occupied Germany. The black marketeers, smuggling coffee and cigarettes from Belgium and Holland, used surplus American Army White scout cars and half-tracks and fought running battles with the German customs men. Between 1945 and 1950, in that same area where 'Lightning Joe' Collins had once tried to capture Aachen, forty smugglers and customs men died in such shootouts.

By the early fifties, however, the frontier started to achieve some sort of peace. Indeed, as if to symbolize the fact that the bloody past was at last being buried, the city of Aachen gave its famed *Karlspreis*★ to that statesman who ten years before had ordered his generals to join him in urinating on the 'Great West Wall of Germany' – Winston Churchill.

It was the beginning. Years later the Americans of that refounded 'Forgotten Army', the Seventh, which is in Germany to this very day, started to come back to those frontier villages where their fathers had

---

★ Named after Charlemagne the Great who is buried in Aachen Cathedral.

fought and died in 1944/45. Now they lived side by side with the Germans as allies and friends.

At last, after a thousand years of war and terror that followed the division of Charlemagne's Empire in 843, the distant border is at peace. The West Wall, as befits an anachronism from another time, has been placed under government protection in some German Federal states. Others have sold the remaining bunkers to private citizens who have planted flowers where 'the bouncing Betty's were once so thickly sown, guarded by those pot-bellied garden dwarves so beloved by the Germans.

'It is a great mistake to return to old battlefields,' someone once wrote, 'as it is to revisit the place of your honeymoon or the house where you grew up. For years you have owned them in your memory. When you go back you find the occupants have rearranged the furniture.'

How true! Those West Wall bunkers which held up Colonel Lanham's 22nd Regiment have now become gentle mounds in an Eifel farmer's backyard. Those dragon's teeth upon which Colonel Doan's tanks of the 3rd Armored were pounded to pulp have disappeared into the firs and are covered with green mould, making them look like oddly regular rocks. Time, progress and the earth itself have drawn an almost impenetrable cloak over those scenes of desperate action where young men fought and died over a half a century ago.

But the Great Wall which Hitler built is still there, all three hundred and fifty miles of it, as if daring Time to destroy its concrete heart. Visit it on a soft summer's day, pushing through the green peace of the forest, and it is hard to believe that murder and mayhem once took place there. Was it here where the terrified young soldiers came streaming back, leaving their dead littering the slope behind, throwing away their weapons in their haste to get away?

But it did happen here: a forgotten tragedy, made up of the dramas and disasters of a lot of men who were not consulted about why they were there and why they should die. They were not asked about the effectiveness of the Broad Front Strategy or the rivalry of their generals for the kudos of final victory. They were simply ordered, without explanation, to attack, even if they were killed in the attempt, just as their opponents were commanded in that time-honoured military phrase to 'defend to the last man and the last bullet'. And for too many of them death came to them on this distant frontier.

INDEX